The history of football cards (and stickers) provides a glorious photographic record of the beautiful game. Purchased at the newsagent, flicked against brick walls, swapped and fought over in the playground, the football card and Panini sticker were the Yu-Gi-Oh and Pokemon cards of the 1960s and 1970s, and are as collectable as their modern-day Japanese equivalents.

George Berry's afro

In *Swap Yer!*, the first ever history of the football card, Rob Jovanovic traces its roots back to the golden era of the cigarette card, charts how we blossomed into a nation of collectors and investigates why, no matter how many cards you purchased, you always ended up with eight swaps of Mick Mills rather than Steve Heighway or Stan Bowles.

Swap Yer!

The Wonderful
World of Football
Cards and
Sticker Albums

Also by Rob Jovanovic

Beck! On A Backwards River

Adventures in Hi-Fi:
The Complete R.E.M.
(with Tim Abbott)

The Ice Hockey Superleague
Yearbook

Forest Giants: The Story of
Nottingham Forest 1975–80

Perfect Sound Forever: The Story
of Pavement

Nirvana: The Recording Sessions

Big Star: The Story of Rock's
Forgotten Band

Kate Bush: The Biography

Fifty Years of the European Cup
and Champions League

Swap Yer!

The Wonderful World of Football Cards and Sticker Albums

Rob Jovanovic

First published in hardback
in Great Britain in 2005
by Orion Books
an imprint of the
Orion Publishing Group Ltd
Orion House, 5 Upper St Martin's
Lane, London WC2H 9EA

10 9 8 7 6 5 4 3 2 1

Every effort has been made to
fulfil requirements with regard to
reproducing copyright material.
The author and publisher will be
glad to rectify any omissions at
the earliest opportunity.

www.orionbooks.co.uk

A CIP catalogue record for
this book is available from the
British Library.

ISBN: 0 75287 312 1

Printed and bound in Great Britain
by Butler & Tanner Ltd, Frome and
London

Checklist

Introduction

If you show almost any man of a certain age a collection of football cards and stickers, you invariably get one or both of the following responses: 'Oh, I remember those!' and 'I wish I'd kept hold of my collection. It would probably be worth something now!'

Like many people born after the late 1950s, I too have vivid recollections of collecting football cards and chewing the brittle piece of pink chewing gum that came in the packet. I also spent a good deal of my after-school time in the 1970s striving, usually in vain, to complete an album of stickers. To do this I would invariably blow all of my pocket money on the day I got it on new stickers and then spend the rest of the week doing deals and swapping my doubles: 'Swap yer two Mick Mills for that Leicester City badge?' I managed to finish a Panini album just once, during the otherwise nondescript 1981–82 season. The weeks spent hunting down those elusive stickers of Manchester City's Tommy Caton, Aston Villa's Des Bremner and the Carlisle United team group still haunt me to this day.

As pocket money became a paper-round salary and records took over as the desirable collectables of choice, my cards and partly filled sticker albums were consigned to the backs of cupboards and boxes in the loft. After completely forgetting about them for many years I was presented with them when my parents moved house and cleared out the attic. My wife wasn't too pleased to get more boxes of my 'junk' deposited on our dining-room table. At first I wasn't overly excited either, but as soon as I opened the first box and began flicking through the stacks of cards the memories came flooding back. Football cards and stickers are hand-held pieces of instant nostalgia. In researching this book I've found that a scary amount of people knew their 1970s card collections so well that they could recite the information from the backs of the cards almost verbatim. I found that I could identify obscure players in an instant by remembering their card and sticker pictures. Unearthing cards from twenty-plus years ago resurrects the sounds and smells of the school yard and those long-forgotten images of reaching up to a newsagent's counter stand to pick out a few packets of stickers.

That, in essence, is the inspiration for this book. I hope that you will also have happy memories revived by leafing through these pages. It may be a cliché, but things were simpler back then. There were fewer distractions for children, and imagination was still an important instinct for us. Unfortunately, many of the games that were invented to turn our card collections into entertainment are lost in the mists of time.

For my wife, and her constant battle against my cluttering up the house, the situation got even worse when I discovered in the mid-1990s that I could track down and buy missing cards on the internet. The new acquisitions always triggered fond memories of flicking cards against walls and standing huddled in the corner of the playground. So for the last decade I've been revisiting and expanding

my collection, and, by default, my childhood. And I'm not alone. Millions of cards change hands each year and collecting is proving to be as popular as ever. Once my thirst for filling in gaps from the 1970s was quenched I went back through the history of football. The fruits of my obsessions are contained within this book. If I had a pound for every time someone opened this volume and thought, 'I remember that set,' I'd be very rich.

As the general collecting of football memorabilia has spiralled out of control over the past fifteen years, the collecting of football cards has followed suit. A number of specialist shops and mail-order outlets have sprung up to meet the ever-rising demand for this collecting genre. The number of card-collecting fairs, football memorabilia meetings, auctions and sales is also growing rapidly. Collectors scan the small ads, fairs and auction rooms for elusive cards to complete those annoyingly imperfect sets. They sometimes concentrate on specific aspects of the game. Some people buy cards only from a particular manufacturer or cards from a certain year. Many concentrate on certain teams or players. If you want a particular Manchester United card it'll probably be harder to find than a Leicester City one! And younger collectors might be surprised to learn that Blackpool and Bolton players from the fifties are much more widely available than their Manchester United and

Chelsea contemporaries. They can also discover, through the wonder of cards, that Bobby Charlton and Ray Wilkins once had hair, or that before 1910 every player had a moustache. Personal grooming of players is just one of many reasons to collect cards. The changing fashions and designs of football kits are also evident, and in many cases hilarious.

A visit to a card fair today will reveal a large room packed with stalls and buyers fighting for elbow room at each stand. And the more collectable football cards of the past 125 years are now making their way into auctions. Cards were specifically produced to be collected, and the fact that they provide a beautiful record of the game's history only adds to their collectability and worth. Today auction houses up and down the country regularly hold specific football-card days. In the United States, early baseball cards have attracted bids of up to $500,000. We're not quite in that league (yet), but the rarest individual football cards are now selling for over £1,000. Complete sets often go for many times that figure. How collectable a card is depends on several factors: its scarcity, its condition, the quality of its design and print, and the person or team that is depicted. As more people get the bug, prices are set to rise even further as the rarest cards become ever harder to find.

Football has been an important thread in the social fabric of Britain over the last 140 years, and the cards that depict the sport's stars are an integral part of the story. No other football collectable shows the changing face of the game as clearly as the humble football card.

Happy collecting!
Rob Jovanovic
July 2005

The Early Years

The Origin of Cards

The earliest known 'collectable' cards originated in France in the 1840s. Within forty years they had spread to most of the Western world. Collectable cards were an extension of business cards that traders gave out to customers. Stores in France began doing the same and made the subtle, but in hindsight crucial, change of printing a picture on the back. So, well over a century before supermarket loyalty cards were introduced, the (mainly female) customers of the Victorian age were being encouraged to return so that they could complete card sets featuring geraniums or the fashions of the day.

As the customers began collecting cards from different stores the idea spread, so that different branches of the same shop would offer cards with an alternate image on the reverse, forcing the desperate collectors to visit all of the company's shops. The final step of what is now seen as an ingenious marketing plan was when individual shops gave out cards with different images on certain days of the week. Customers were therefore encouraged to keep returning to the store on what might otherwise have been quiet days of the week to collect all the cards.

Such was the success of this promotional scheme that other industries took note and began using cards as an incentive for buying their products. In Spain cards were given away inside chocolate wrappers, and when the idea spread across the Atlantic US cigarette manufacturers began using cards, too. The first cards to be issued with cigarettes were produced in the 1870s. Cigarettes were ideal for this marketing technique because way back when they were sold not in packets but in flimsy envelopes. To stop the cigarettes being broken, these envelopes had a piece of card inserted to stiffen the packaging.

Cigarette cards were soon a phenomenon in the United States, so much so that the practice of giving away a card inside each packet quickly returned across the Atlantic. The use of picture cards instead of just a plain white board was a massive hit among consumers. But images of flowers and pretty dresses wouldn't suffice for this crowd, because the vast majority of smokers were men. So the cigarette cards' subjects tended to be actresses, militaria and sportsmen. The market was huge: in the USA, the Duke Company claimed to make two million sales a day. The first British cards were issued by the Wills Company of Bristol in 1893, with ships and cricketers among the first subjects.

Within a decade hundreds of cigarette companies were producing cards around the world. The brand loyalty that collecting cards ensured was undeniable. 'That was one of the most brilliant marketing tools ever imagined,' specialist dealer Jay Brannan told *The Times* in 2004.

The First Football Cards

When the UK was first grasping the potential of cigarette cards, the world of football was just starting to blossom, too. The Football League had been founded in 1888 with twelve teams. A decade later there were two divisions of eighteen teams each. Professionalism within the game had been legalised and crowds were rising. The first FA Cup Final in 1872 had drawn 2,000 curious spectators to see the Wanderers beat the Royal Engineers by a single goal. For the 1898 final, over 62,000 packed into Crystal Palace to watch Nottingham Forest beat Derby County 3–1.

The first football-related card is officially recognised as being of Liverpool FC captain D. McLean. It is widely accepted that it appeared in 1890. But, like many of the early issues, this card is subject to much confusion and speculation. Issued by Field Favorites Cigarettes (note the US spelling), the series was not numbered and only this solitary card has ever been recorded.

The Singleton & Cole's cards shown here can each fetch £120 on the open market. Note the formal attire and the disinterested look on England international Steve Bloomer's face. He was well known for being nonchalant about his goal-scoring ability. The cigarettes were marketed as 'high grade', and the rear of the card makes the claim that 'All these cigarettes are guaranteed absolutely pure and free from dust.'

Whether any other footballers were included in the set is unknown. It's strange that the captain of a team from the lowly Lancashire League was chosen as the subject of such a ground-breaking card, but, more importantly for collectors, the supposed date of 1890 must be wrong: Liverpool Football Club did not even exist until 1892. Nevertheless, on the rare occasions that Mr McLean becomes available, he fetches well over £1,000.

In 1897, the London firm Cohen, Weenan and Co. included over 40 footballers in their 100-card set *Heroes of Sport*. This exponential rise in the use of footballers was mirroring the game's nation-wide rise in popularity at the turnstiles. Long-disused team names like Woolwich Arsenal, Small Heath, Casuals and Corinthians feature heavily among this series. Ogden's of Liverpool were soon using their Guinea Gold cigarettes to issue thousands of cards, many of which featured football subjects. These are quite hard to track down and exactly how many were issued (and of whom) is unclear. The same company's Tabs brand gave out 25 football cards in 1902, but in that year Wills and Glasgow's J & F Bell produced a much more exciting, football-only set. At the time it was still a novelty to see pictures of players (newspapers did not yet print photographs and of course this was long before cinema and TV), so cards of the stars were sure to set pulses racing. The Bell set was simply titled *Footballers*

and featured 30 international stars of the early twentieth century. Head-and-shoulder photographs of the players wearing their Sunday-best jackets and ties with stiff collared shirts emphasised the still-gentlemanly nature of the game at this point in its history.

In 1901 American tobacco companies tried to muscle in on the burgeoning UK market, which prompted the British firms to unite under the banner of the Imperial Tobacco Company. By now, the most popular method of gaining a share of the huge smokers' market was the use of cards. Brian Asquith, a consultant at Bonham's auction house, explains the scale of the enterprise: 'Every town had a cigarette factory and each produced cigarette cards. That means that you have some card runs that were nation-wide, and ran into the millions, and some that were tiny and covered just one town. All important events were recorded on cigarette cards and the early ones carried the most stunning designs. Some were decorated on the back as well as the front. As mass production developed, the quality declined until, by the 1930s, they were producing runs of three or four million cards, which would be worth only a few pounds today. But single cards from the early runs can be worth over a thousand pounds now.'

Football Expands

The largest of the early football sets was Taddy's *Prominent Footballers*, which provided the first really wide-ranging pictorial documentation of the sport, with almost 600 players depicted. Taddy was one of the most respected cigarette firms, a reputation they gained partly because of the high quality of their cards. There is also an air of mystery about the company. It had formed way back in 1740, but after 180 years of trading it disappeared almost overnight. In 1920 the workers announced that they were going on strike to show solidarity with employees at another company. The Taddy management said they would be forced to close if the strike went ahead, but the workforce called their bosses' bluff and walked out. Immediately the factories were locked, never to reopen, much to the shock of the workers.

Founded in 1848, Cope Bros., a family-run Liverpool company, had bought out several competitors by the turn of the century. They were equally ambitious where cards were concerned. There were now 40 league teams and Cope's were determined to feature them all, so the company's *Noted Footballers* set included a whopping 470 players inserted in their Clips brand of cigarettes.

As more colour was used in card production, the companies often issued sets in club colours to provide as engaging a set of cards as possible. Ogden's *Club Colours* in 1906 and *Famous Footballers* in 1908 were two of the most colourful early sets. These sets now provide an interesting peek into the kits that various clubs wore in their early days. Watford's Rastafarian hoops of green, red and gold take some beating, but other clubs were turning out in drastically different colours, too. Bristol Rovers wore black and white stripes, QPR's hoops were green and white, while Aberdeen had shirts of black and gold stripes.

Many football shirts seem quite alien to the colours and designs of today. You'll probably not see a goalkeeper donning a flat-cap either. The oval designs of the Clips and *Prominent Footballers* cards are reminiscent of the miniatures that might have been kept in lockets at the time.

GALLAHER'S CIGARETTES.

WM. YENSON,
CROYDON COMMON, 1909-10.

COPE'S
"CLIPS"
CIGARETTES

NO. 41.—DERRICK
Notts Forest
Noted Footballers

PROMINENT FOOTBALLERS.

R. WARD,
SUNDERLAND.

BOLTON WANDERERS.

The Most Expensive Football Cigarette Cards

(If you see any of these sets for sale at a car-boot sale, snap them up quickly!)

Company	Series (year of issue)	Price per card
Rutherford's	Footballers (1900)	£1000.00
Field Favorites	Footballers (1893)	£750.00
Spiro Valleri	Noted Footballers (1908)	£500.00
Hunter	Footballers (1910)	£500.00
Robert Sinclair	Footballers (1900)	£400.00
St Petersburg	Footballers (1900)	£400.00
Casket Tobacco	Fixture Cards (1909)	£350.00
Hook of Holland	Footballers (1900)	£250.00
Brigham & Co.	Reading Players (1912)	£200.00
W. T. Davies	Newport F.C. (1904)	£200.00

Early Football Postcards

In the early twentieth century, the main method of communication was via the humble postcard. Millions were sent, and they are now collectable in their own right. Of course, football was sometimes the subject on the card, as the two distinct examples (shown on the previous page) illustrate. The first shows a goalkeeper wearing the same shirt as the outfield players and heading the ball clear; while the second, from Spain, features a photographed goal-mouth action shot.

'They cost a halfpenny to send. Every London postbox was emptied every hour and the post was delivered five or six times a day,' explains Brian Asquith. 'This meant that you could send a note to your sister telling her that you would be coming around for tea that afternoon and a note to the butcher asking him to prepare a joint of beef for collection later. On top of that, every Edwardian household had an album in which to keep their collection of postcards. Every small town had its own photographer, who would capture local events – accidents were especially popular – and anyone in the news would appear on the cards.'

The First Football Superstars and Cricketing Footballers

Other early twentieth-century cards showed the overlapping careers of cricketers and footballers. S. H. Wood played both sports at the top level, while Everton's Harry Makepeace was also a Test cricketer for England. Andrew Ducat, shown right in 1922, was an 'international footballer and England cricketer.' Later, Denis and Les Compton played for Arsenal and Middlesex (the former also won England caps in both sports), while more recently Geoff Hurst turned out for Essex and Ian Botham played football for Scunthorpe.

Though card collections were mainly accumulated by men, children were often given them by their fathers, and gangs of kids could be seen outside tobacconists asking customers for their cards as they left the shops. The early football superstars were idolised by children even though they rarely saw them in the flesh: few could even afford to watch their local team and the days of ubiquitous televised matches were far in the future.

Comedy Cards

Cards didn't just show action shots or player portraits. The laws of the game and the age's sense of humour were also depicted. Here we see some puns on *Football Terms*. Much of this set featured both Association and Rugby Football codes.

ANDREW DUCAT.

Over the bar.

GRENADIER CIGARETTES
W. & F. Faulkner Lᵗᵈ. London, s.e.
COPYRIGHT.

Scrimmage.

GRENADIER CIGARETTES
W. & F. Faulkner Lᵗᵈ. London, s.e.
COPYRIGHT.

A good pass.

GRENADIER CIGARETTES
W. & F. Faulkner Lᵗᵈ. London, s.e.
COPYRIGHT.

Early Internationals

As smoking was such a massive, lucrative industry, the various companies were in heated battles for the biggest share of the market. The quality of the card was taken as an indication of the quality of the product, so, with manufacturers constantly attempting to outdo their rivals, designs and reproduction techniques embraced the latest technology. Printing was carried out throughout the UK and, before the First World War, in hi-tech Germany, too. Advances in printing such as Letterpress, Lithography and Photogravure were all seized upon by the tobacco companies as the cards became ever more enticing. Letterpress used a raised surface to imprint the ink on to the cards; Lithography used a flat surface; and Photogravure used a recessed surface. Letterpress was the most widely used process during the 1930s. The Churchman's *Association Footballers* on pages 37–39 show this method in all its glory. Photogravure was used by many companies to give a card a photo-real front with a shade of brown to it. In the vast majority of cases the backs of cards were printed with a single colour to save on costs.

But the card-backs were not neglected as the text became increasingly detailed and informative. A full set of cards from a particular season gives a fascinating insight into the history of the game and a delightful visual record unsurpassed in other media. Early internationals attained massive prestige, so players photographed in their international shirts and caps were especially desirable.

The First World War

By the 1910s the collecting of football cards had really taken off. This was the Edwardian Age, and team photos show trainers and managers in bowler hats and straw boaters. The league was flourishing and the times were good. But in August 1914 Britain declared war on Germany. At home it was claimed that the war would be over by Christmas, so the football season was launched as planned. The Churchman Company of Portman Road in Ipswich put out a pleasing series, *Footballers*, in November 1914. But by the end of the season the war was no nearer its conclusion and the Football League was suspended. Smaller regional competitions continued, but many players boarded ships bound for the fighting in France and Belgium.

Football card production was also suspended as paper stocks dwindled. The only set known to be issued before the end of the war appeared in 1917 when F & J Smith produced *Football Club Records*.

Right: Sam Chedgzoy of Everton proudly wearing his 1920 England cap.

Below: These cards truly bring home the human cost of the war. Some players have the letters 'OHMS' beneath their names, indicating that they are On His Majesty's Service, in one of the armed forces. Other cards are more chilling: they have the simple caption 'Died of wounds' on the front.

S. CHEDGZOY.

F. & J. SMITH'S CIGARETTES

AIRDRIEONIANS.
J. REID,
O.H.M.S.

F. & J. SMITH'S CIGARETTES

QUEEN'S PARK.
E. S. GARVIE,
DIED OF WOUNDS.

F. & J. SMITH'S CIGARETTES

THIRD LANARK.
J. BROWNLIE,
O.H.M.S.

Between the Wars

Godfrey Phillips' *Pinnace* Series

Football cards were slow to re-emerge after the war, although the Godfrey Phillips Company produced a football-only set of 'silks' in 1920. (It had produced a similar series in 1914.) These were literally pieces of silk which had the colours of each club printed on to the cloth. They were given away in cigarette packets, and are now highly collectable.

The first major foray back into football cards was made by the same firm. Between 1920 and 1924 it produced what is still the most wide-ranging snapshot of the British football world: the mammoth *Pinnace Footballers* series. Over these four seasons they released cards featuring 2,462 different players from all manner of leagues across England and Scotland, and even threw in a handful of rugby players.

Even more mind-boggling is that many of the players were issued several times across the different seasons. Furthermore, the backs of the cards have design variations as a result of the various printers that were employed by Phillips. At least five different backs are known, so the complete set must actually comprise something like 10,000 individual cards!

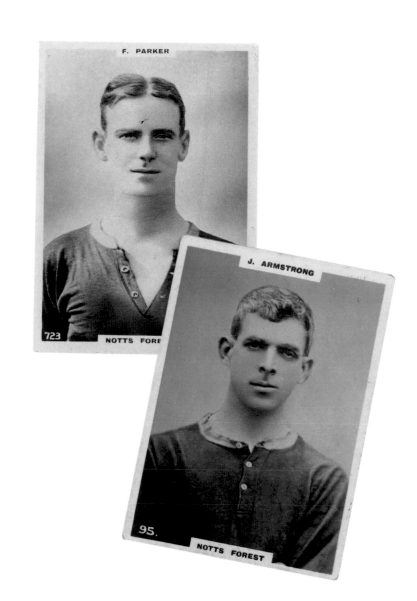

F. PARKER

723

NOTTS FORE[ST]

J. ARMSTRONG

95.

NOTTS FOREST

The cards were relatively small, measuring approximately 3.5 x 4.5 cm, and featured a simple black-and-white, head-and-shoulders photograph of the player concerned. These are often the only photographic records of many of the players.

In the early 1920s the UK had many millions of heavy smokers, so the cards were collected at an astonishing rate. Once 25 of the standard small cards had been collected they could be exchanged for one larger card (the size of a modern-day gum card). When you had 10 of these you could exchange them for an even larger card listed as 'cabinet sized'. So to get a team set of 11 of the largest cards, you would have smoked the small matter of 55,000 cigarettes!

Boys' Comics and Papers

Boys' newspapers and comics enjoyed a boom in the 1920s, and gave children the chance to obtain cards of their sporting heroes without the need to buy a packet of cigarettes. Publishers D. C. Thomson and the Amalgamated Press were prolific in this area, with cards being given out 'with the editor's compliments' every week. *Boys' Friend, Sport and Adventure, Boys' Realm, Champion* and *Boys' Magazine* were just some of the titles involved. The cards usually had the name of periodical printed on them, and for a while the date and issue number appeared on the reverse, along with a preview of what was coming next week. As the same card was given away in every issue for a particular week many of these cards were printed, and consequently they are relatively inexpensive to collect today.

The comics also experimented with other ways of giving its readers something to collect. *Champion* issued a small album (see overleaf) which contained players' pictures but left spaces for the kids to cut out and paste in facsimile autographs from the comic each week. *Boys' Magazine* issued a similar mini-album which could hold colour action pictures distributed on a sheet each week. A cynical observer might criticise the comics for enticing young children with the hook of a free card each week, but at least the products were of good quality.

Fashions of the day were just as changeable back then as they are today. Note the differing approach to wearing a shirt. 'Tucked or un-tucked?', that was the question.

F. MOSS

B. MENLOVE

SAM CHEDGZOY

G. WILSON

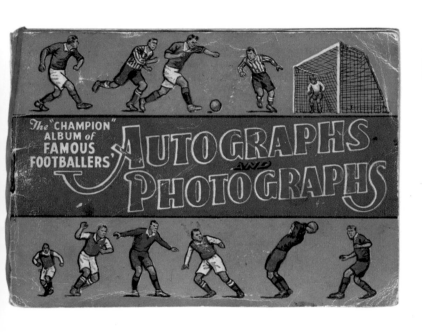

The "CHAMPION" ALBUM of FAMOUS FOOTBALLERS' AUTOGRAPHS AND PHOTOGRAPHS

TOPICAL TIMES

ALBUM OF
GREAT
PLAYERS

CLOSE-UPS
OF THE
STARS

PRESENTED WITH TOPICAL TIMES

Rules and Innovations /
Tactics and Formations

From its earliest days the football card has been a vehicle for the explanation of rules and tactics. Cards on the continent displayed formations and pitch markings (as in these French and Spanish examples), while John Player & Sons produced the 50-card *Hints on Association Football* which eventually amounted to a valuable handbook covering all aspects of the game.

TRIANGULAR WING MOVEMENT

WHEN NOT TO SHOOT

The *Triangular Wing Movement* card attempts to resurrect a well-used ploy that had been exploited before the offside rule was changed in the 1924–5 season. Previously three opponents (usually the goalkeeper plus two defenders) had been required for a player to remain onside. In this season it was reduced to the present-day two players.

Cup Winners /
The John Player Company

By 1877 John Player, a former agricultural supplier, had seen so much potential in the cigarette market that he purchased a factory in Nottingham and formed the John Player Company.

The firm issued a host of innovative and distinctive football sets in the early twentieth century, and several series that really captured the atmosphere of the Roaring Twenties. The well-drawn caricatures by artists 'Mac' (Douglas Machin) and 'Rip' (R. Hill) were certainly of their time. In 1930 the company produced the 50-card *Association Cup Winners* series. This set covered every FA Cup-winning side since 1883, when the short-lived Blackburn Olympic had captured the trophy.

ENSEÑANZA DEL
JUEGO DE FOOT-BALL ASOCIACIÓN

CHOCOLATE·AMATLLER

CHOCOLATE·AMATLLER

COLECCIÓN DE 25 DIBUJOS

N.º 1   Uniforme de los equipos

Entrada de un defensa

Deben cuidar las defensas de cortar
todo ataque de sus contrarios. Esto es,
impedir, utilizando todos los medios le-
gales, que sus contrarios hagan goal.

Cuando sus compañeros dominan pue-
den adelantarse hacia el campo contrario
pero con mucha precaución y siempre
uno más adelantado que otro, pues no
deben abandonar nunca su goal.

La línea de defensa la componen dos
jugadores, defensa derecha y defensa iz-
quierda.

CHOCOLATE
AMATLLE
Casa fundada
en 1800
BARCELONA

ENSEÑANZA DEL JUEGO DE FOOT-BALL (ASOCIACIÓN)

CHOCOLATE·AMATLLER

CHOCOLATE·AMATLLER

N.º 6   Entrada de un defensa

Spanish Chocolate Issues

As football cards spread across Europe all manner of products issued them to encourage customer loyalty. This set of Spanish cards from the early 1930s was issued in Amataller chocolate and is therefore quite hard to find without some signs of the combination of chocolate and children's fingers! It covered all aspects of the game, from tactics and formations to dimensions of the pitch.

It's amazing how one's hobby can inadvertently supply you with a subconscious, seemingly laser-guided homing device for finding gems in the unlikeliest locations. During a 2004 trip to Barcelona I was shopping with my wife in the old-town district which contained the usual assortment of gift shops, restaurants and local craft emporiums. So you can imagine my delight, and my wife's resignation, when I discovered a specialist card dealership tucked away in the narrow, dusty streets. Half an hour later my wife had been provided with a chair while I was surrounded by shoeboxes full of rare, and expensive, Spanish cards. The only problem was that I couldn't speak a word of Spanish and the large but friendly shopkeeper couldn't speak a word of English. Haggling was done via scraps of paper and eventually I was ready to pay a small fortune, only to find out that he didn't accept plastic. Most helpfully, he drew me a complicated map to the local cashpoint. I'm currently learning Spanish for any future trips.

Early Team Photos

Cigarette cards enjoyed their golden age in the 1920s and 1930s. The Ardath Tobacco Company was selling quality cigarettes which were among the most fashionable available. While the *Pinnace* set had covered every level of British football from Aberdare Athletic and South Shields to Manchester United and Glasgow Rangers, Ardath issued over 700 team-photo cards in the mid-1930s. One packet might contain a local amateur side and the next a First Division giant. The teams were issued in five 110-card series covering Lancashire, Yorkshire, the North East, the Midlands and the South, as well as Scotland (which had 165 cards). Prices for these high-quality photo cards range from about £1.20 to £2, which isn't bad for a single card. But to collect, say, Yorkshire, would set you back about £160. And you'd still have five regions to go!

Early Albums

The Wills Company produced generic albums that could be used for whichever series of cards you desired, but they also issued set-specific albums like this *Association Footballers* one from the 1935–36 season. Some of their albums provided slots to hold the cards in place without the need for any

SHEFFIELD UNITED F.C.

LEYTONSTONE FOOTBALL CLUB

LIVERPOOL F.C.

"SMOKE THE BEST" "ISLANDERS" "FAGS" "SPECIALS" "CLUBS" "ALL PURE VIRGINIA"

No. 24.   LIVERPOOL F.C., 1923-4.

Wadsworth (Trainer), MacNab, Scott, Walsh, Lillie, Bromilow,

Longworth, Gillespy, Foreshaw, McKinlay (Capt.) Chambers, Hopkin.

adhesive, while others required you to glue them (instantly slashing their value for collectors seventy years down the line).

Leafing through these albums today transports you to a different era. The Hull City goalkeeper G. Madison is described as having 'shrewd and original ideas' but we are not told what they were. Stanley Matthews reveals that he started young: 'I was always at it at school in Hanley and I was given a job on the Stoke ground when I was 16.' We also discover that West Brom's centre-forward W. Boyes was only 5 feet 4 inches tall and was scouted while playing for the Woodhouse Mill United team. Visually, the cards are stunning, with excellent, full-colour photos showing greased-back hair and collars that would have made Elvis envious.

During the late 1920s, several cigarette firms tried to woo buyers by offering points cards. When enough points had been saved you could trade them in for exciting gifts, such as a hand-mirror or even an article of clothing. Competition between companies grew fierce. Ever more expensive gift inducements were offered, but sanity eventually prevailed and in 1933 it was agreed to halt all of these schemes. Picture cards again became the only inserts in packets of cigarettes.

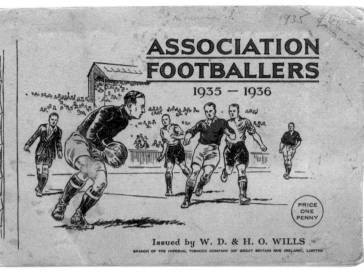

ASSOCIATION FOOTBALLERS
1935 — 1936

PRICE ONE PENNY

Issued by W. D. & H. O. WILLS

BRANCH OF THE IMPERIAL TOBACCO COMPANY (OF GREAT BRITAIN AND IRELAND), LIMITED

E. F. BROOK *(Manchester City)*. Daring and original in style, and claiming the licence to roam into all sorts of unusual positions, Brook has had a distinguished career since he left Barnsley to play for Manchester City in season 1927–'28 at the same time as his colleague, Tilson. As an outside-left he stakes all on the element of surprise, and he has gained many goals by stealing inside and taking opponents unawares. He has appeared in two Cup Finals, securing a winner's medal in 1934. He first played for England in 1930, and has been capped on twelve occasions (including matches against foreign countries). (No. 7)

H. CARTER *(Sunderland)* was a fine all-round athlete as a schoolboy in Sunderland, winning distinction in cricket, swimming and athletics, and playing against the Welsh and Scottish boys in 1927. He quickly qualified for a place in the Sunderland team on becoming a professional. Indeed, while still in his teens, he became an outstanding inside forward, capable of playing on either the right or left wing. In the 1934–'35 season he played brilliantly for his club, and was a big factor in the struggle to wrest the League championship from the Arsenal. He has twice played for England against Scotland—in 1934, and in the Jubilee match in Aug. 1935. (No. 8)

J. CONNOR *(Sunderland)* was born in Renfrew, and crossed the border in 1930, having previously served his apprenticeship with Paisley Celtic and Glasgow Pertshire. He first became a professional in 1926 with St. Mirren, from whom Sunderland secured his transfer, and in the meantime he has gained the highest honours for Scotland. Although he likes to work the ball mainly with his left foot, Connor does not allow this to be a handicap, and in the 1934–'35 season he was one of the most brilliant outside-lefts in the game, playing a big part in the success of the Sunderland side. In the new type of modern wing play he is a grand marksman. (No. 9)

Football cards could be found everywhere across Europe. Here we see some examples from the German Monopol-Dresden cigarette company.

The Peak of Cigarette Cards and Beyond

Card culture progressed until a 1930s urban myth circulated that some First Division managers would buy a new player only if he was featured on a cigarette card. In this decade it seemed that everyone in the country was a smoker, and over 10,000 different football cards were issued before the start of the Second World War. The closer you look at the faces, kits and action scenes on the cards, and read the descriptions on the back, the closer you get to understanding what those days were like.

Football was far from the only subject for cigarette cards, though. Other sets included such eclectic topics as *Public School Ties*, *Famous Escapes*, *Household Hints* and *How to Make a Valve Amplifier*.

In the 1920s the first collecting clubs had been formed up and down the country. While some people thought it was immoral and unethical to buy cards that had been given out as free gifts, many were prepared to pay for them in order to complete sets. The London Cigarette Company even began issuing guides to complete sets. This was the Holy Grail for any collector: the hallowed checklist. Now you not only had a handy guide to all the cards, but another card with which you could keep track of them.

WILLS'S CIGARETTES

S. MATTHEWS (STOKE CITY)

C. BASTIN

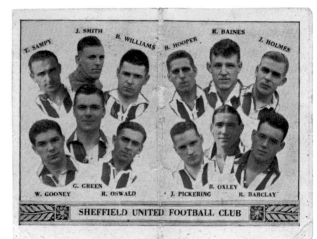

T. SAMPY · J. SMITH · B. WILLIAMS · B. HOOPER · R. BAINES · J. HOLMES · G. GREEN · W. COONEY · R. OSWALD · J. PICKERING · B. OXLEY · R. BARCLAY

SHEFFIELD UNITED FOOTBALL CLUB

SHEFFIELD UNITED

The year 1889 saw the seeds of a great football club sown. Shoots soon appeared, four years later they were runners-up in the Second Division, then twice in Division I, and in 1898 the Championship of the First was theirs. The next year a stout branch was added, the Cup was won; again three years after and still twice more, in 1915 and 1925, making four successes in all. Colours: Red and white with black knickers.

ISSUED BY

BARRATT & CO. LTD.
WOOD-GREEN, LONDON, ENG.

ENGLISH LEAGUE
Division I.

SHEFFIELD
UNITED

The Second World War

The outbreak of war once again brought an end to cigarette card production because paper had to be conserved. However, in marked contrast to after the First World War, it never resumed, despite the clamouring of collectors. In 1939 card production had been at its peak, with Churchman's second series of *Association Footballers* issued in September, and Wills' second series of *Association Footballers* following two months later.

The war led to numerous football-related tragedies. One of many players not to return was Leeds United's E. Stephenson. Others simply could not regain their form having missed five or more seasons of football. The reconstruction after hostilities had ceased included work on pitches and stands that had been bombed. Major rivals like Arsenal and Spurs and the two Mancunian teams shared grounds until they could stand on their own two feet again. But cigarette cards never recovered. Maybe young boys had found that collecting bits of shrapnel during the war was more exciting than collecting cards.

The closest we came to a revival were Carrera's 'Turf slides', which were images printed directly on to cigarette packets. Many collectors found these unappealing, though, as they had to be cut out from the box. Packets containing ten cigarettes provided one slide, with two appearing on packs of twenty. The first set appeared in 1948 and featured head-and-shoulders portraits, while the second (from 1951) comprised a series of impressive caricatures. Today the uncut slides are very collectable.

The Barrett Company started putting cards in sweet cigarette packets in 1947, seizing on the gap in the market left by the real cigarette manufacturers. By the 1950s cards were well and truly back, but while cigarette manufacturers had aimed their cards at adult collectors, the confectioners pitched theirs directly at children.

In the new decade cards would be given away with chewing gum, sweets, biscuits and even packets of tea. To help complete collections, vouchers could be sent in from the products in exchange for the missing cards. A new boom in collecting helped establish these new initiatives, and tens of thousands of cards have been published since. With children getting direct access to cards for the first time, a whole new generation of collectors was born. They not only featured every boy's favourite sports – football and cricket – but were also a social tool because you could swap them with your friends. They were also highly addictive: you simply *had* to finish a set.

20 "TURF" 20

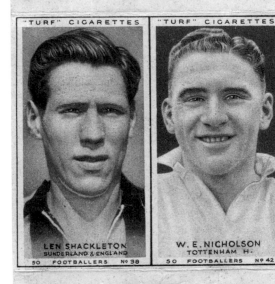

"TURF" CIGARETTES

"TURF" CIGARETTES

LEN SHACKLETON
SUNDERLAND & ENGLAND

50   FOOTBALLERS   No 38

W. E. NICHOLSON
TOTTENHAM H.

50   FOOTBALLERS   No 42

20 "TURF" 20

Churchman's *Association Footballers*, 1938.

CHURCHMAN'S CIGARETTES

W. McDONALD (COVENTRY CITY)

CHURCHMAN'S CIGARETTES

E. HAPGOOD (ARSENAL)

CHURCHMAN'S CIGARETTES

S. CULLIS
(WOLVERHAMPTON WANDERERS)

CHURCHMAN'S CIGARETTES

D. McCULLOCH (BRENTFORD)

CHURCHMAN'S CIGARETTES

E. COLEMAN (NORWICH CITY)

CHURCHMAN'S CIGARETTES

A. BEATTIE (PRESTON NORTH END)

CHURCHMAN'S CIGARETTES

R. DIX (DERBY COUNTY)

CHURCHMAN'S CIGARETTES

P. BUCHANAN (CHELSEA)

CHURCHMAN'S CIGARETTES

H. BETMEAD (GRIMSBY TOWN)

CHURCHMAN'S CIGARETTES

L. GOULDEN (WEST HAM UNITED)

CHURCHMAN'S CIGARETTES

W. HUGHES (BIRMINGHAM)

CHURCHMAN'S CIGARETTES

B. JONES
(WOLVERHAMPTON WANDERERS)

CHURCHMAN'S CIGARETTES

A. McNAB (WEST BROMWICH ALBION)

CHURCHMAN'S CIGARETTES

J. LAWTON (EVERTON)

CHURCHMAN'S CIGARETTES

P. DOHERTY (MANCHESTER CITY)

CHURCHMAN'S CIGARETTES

A. KEEPING (FULHAM)

CHURCHMAN'S CIGARETTES

W. M'KAY (MANCHESTER UNITED)

CHURCHMAN'S CIGARETTES

S. MATTHEWS (STOKE CITY)

The 1950s and Gum Cards

Master Vending

The Master Vending Machine Company of Cricklewood Lane epitomised the new style of gum cards that emerged in the 1950s. They produced just eight sets of cards during 1958 and 1959 then vanished from the card scene, but they left a wonderful, if short-lived, legacy. Gum cards were around three times the size of the old cigarette cards and felt much sturdier in your hands. This was mainly because you bought the cards directly and wanted to have something substantial for your money, whereas cigarette cards had been free gifts.

The *Cardmaster Football Tips* was a triumph of simple design, featuring stylish line drawings of the day's top players with engaging football tips on the reverse. However, the set is quite frustrating for collectors as slight discrepancies in the colours of the card backs and different players being given the same card number often make it impossible to complete a full set covering all the variations.

Top Tips from Master Vending *Cardmaster Football Tips*

1. Hard Grounds: 'Sprinkle boracic powder in your stockings and this will help you to reach the ideal standard of play.'

2. Football Boots: 'One quick method to break them in is to put on a pair of woollen socks with the toes and heels smeared with soft soap. Then lace the boots up and soak them in warm water.'

3. Tackling from Behind: 'Pursue the forward and when nearly level with him shoot out your foot in front of the ball. The ball will be trapped and he will fall over it.'

4. Dribbling: 'Don't have your ankles stiff, but flexible and persuade the ball rather than kick it.'

5. Important Points for Wing-Forwards: 'Always use your pace and never dribble backwards.'

6. Trapping: 'Don't stamp on the ball, but rather let the ball hit your foot as it starts to rise.'

7. Food: 'On no account whatsoever should you have a heavy meal before you are due to go out on the field of play. It is not at all good that your digestive system should be at work and put to such hard gruelling as you throw your body about it into all kinds of strenuous physical endeavour.'

NAT LOFTHOUSE

BOLTON & ENGLAND

GEORGE FARM

BLACKPOOL & SCOTLAND

STANLEY MATTHEWS

BLACKPOOL & ENGLAND

Cardmaster Football Tips
SERIES OF 50. CARD No. 18

Trapping

Allow the ball to drop just in front of you or a little to one side then as it reaches the ground and is just beginning to rise place your foot carefully but firmly on it and don't allow it to bounce more than a few inches from your foot. Don't stamp on the ball, but rather let the ball hit your foot as it starts to rise.

The Master Vending Machine Co. Ltd.
82-106 Cricklewood Lane, London. NW2

Gum Cards and Albums

In the 1950s another marketing breakthrough came when companies realised that instead of just giving away cards with various commodities they could sell packs directly, usually with a complimentary stick of bubblegum included. During the 1950s there was an air of prosperity around the country. Rationing had ended and exciting new items were being offered for sale. The first TVs found their way into households during the decade and people had money to spend for the first time in years.

Soccer Gum, Chix Bubble Gum and A & BC were at the forefront of this new way of distributing cards. Soccer Gum, for example, produced two 48-card sets of colourful team pictures in 1956 and 1958, each covering a wide range of clubs from Doncaster Rovers and Accrington Stanley to Arsenal and Everton.

Clevedon Confectionery produced what is now a highly desirable set of Football Club Managers which included a young Bill Shankly at Huddersfield. In a 2003 auction a set of these 50 cards reached a staggering £2,000!

Peter Adolph used cards to help market his fledgling Subbuteo table football game in 1952.

No. 33 DAVID WALSH
(Aston Villa and Ireland)

Born in Waterford, Eire, David Walsh started his career with Limerick, later joined Linfield. Signed by West Bromwich Albion in 1946. Scored a century of goals for them before being transferred to Villa. Capped many times for Eire. Ideally built for a centre-forward. Lost his place to Derek Pace.

No. 34 SAMMY COX
(Rangers and Scotland)

Left back for Scotland for many years, Cox has been the man to face the menace of either Stan Matthews or Tom Finney. No back could play the maestros better than this Rangers' stalwart. One of the best backs ever to have represented his country.

Chix Bubble Gum
FOOTBALL
PICTURE ALBUM

SOCCER
PICTURE CARD ALBUM

JOHN CHARLES

DENNIS LAW

A & BC

American & British Chewing Gum Limited, a.k.a. A & BC, became the UK arm of American card and gum giants Topps. In the early 1950s they joined the growing ranks of companies issuing cards with a stick of bubblegum in each packet. At this time, having a lower jaw resembling that of a feasting cow was fast becoming the essential fashion accessory of all wannabe Teddy Boys and Rock'n'Rollers. Bubblegum was the epitome of American cool. Girls in bobby socks and boys in leather jackets could be seen chewing by the soda fountain in any number of Hollywood movies. This was the birth of teen culture from across the Pond.

A & BC issued card series featuring Elvis, The Beatles (expect to pay £10 per card for the 1964 coloured series) and The Monkees. They also kept up with the latest TV shows, putting out sets of *Batman* and later *The Planet of the Apes*. But their longest-running series came in the form of a wide-ranging collection of football cards between the 1958–59 and 1974–75 seasons.

Right from the very beginning A & BC provided collectors with the joys, and associated headaches, of variations on their core set of cards. The 1958–59 *Footballers* set was sized roughly at what would become the standard football card dimensions; gone were the days of fiddly little cards. They were also brightly coloured, with head-and-shoulders portraits of 46 players, each against a vivid background. But then the variations kicked in. These cards were issued in two different picture sizes, two different colours of ink on the back (blue and black), and some had a cut-off slip on the front which pointed out that collectors could obtain an album by writing to 50 Hampstead Road NW1.

As if that wasn't enough, they then issued a second 46-card series later in the same season with many of the same variations and an added one of some cards not having the club crest on the front. Variations of this sort might seem inconsequential to the casual buyer, but they can mean a price difference of £5 per card to a serious collector. They also mean that instead of collecting 92 cards to complete the set you could be chasing the best part of 500 to have every version of each card! And this is for just one season.

The backs of A & BC cards came to be almost as important as the fronts. Well-researched biographies of the players, quizzes and player stats were all crammed in. For instance, we could find out that Bobby Robson's nickname was 'Nipper' and that Don Revie's burning ambition was to play in the Amateur Open golf championship.

The following season was less complicated for collectors, and the company also helped out by

issuing two checklist cards featuring team photos of the FA Cup holders (Nottingham Forest) and reigning League Champions (Wolves). This time the set comprised 98 cards and boasted the innovation of a quiz on the rear of each card. When you thought you knew the answer you had to rub a 'blank' space with the edge of a coin to reveal the answer. What tension must have ensued if you had any coins left after buying the cards and chewing the gum.

DONALD REVIE - SUNDERLAND

ROBERT WILLIAM ROBSON — W.B.A.

ROBERT WILLIAM (NIPPER) ROBSON

7

Born in Langley Park, Durham. He signed for Fulham in 1950 and in 1956 was transferred to West Bromwich Albion for £25,000. Before the World Cup series last year he had two full international caps and one-B international cap. Height 5 feet 10½ inches, weight 11 stone 9 pounds. He is a very forceful and fast running inside forward, scoring many goals for his club. He has played right and left half, outside right, inside right, centre forward and inside left during his professional career but his favourite position is inside right. His twin ambitions are to appear in a Cup Final and to play in an England World Cup winning team. His favourite sportsman is Tom Finney.

Which Welsh international full back started as an amateur with Wrexham?

Answer

Stewart Grenville Williams,—West Bromwich Albion.

A & B C

Printed in England

edwin holliday

Outside-left

MIDDLESBROUGH
& ENGLAND

ron moran

Left-back

LIVERPOOL

jock davidson

Right-back

HULL CITY

bobby brennan

Outside-left

NORWICH CITY
& IRELAND

jimmy armfield

Right-back

BLACKPOOL
& ENGLAND

ronnie clayton

Right-half

BLACKBURN ROVERS
& ENGLAND

derek sullivan

Wing-half

CARDIFF CITY
& WALES

stan matthews

Outside-right

BLACKPOOL
& ENGLAND

A & BC 1958–59

GEORGE COHEN

DAVE MACKAY

TOTTENHAM H. & SCOTLAND

NAT LOFTHOUSE

BOLTON W. & ENGLAND

JOHNNY HAYNES

JOHN MOLYNEUX

LIVERPOOL

JIMMY HILL

FULHAM

R. CHARLTON

MANCHESTER UNITED & ENGLAND

BILLY WRIGHT

LATE OF WOLVES & ENGLAND

A & BC 1959–60

H1	Ferenc Puskas

HUNGARY — REAL MADRID

The galloping major. 1953 saw him humiliate England with a brand of skill never before seen in this country. The best left foot I have ever seen. Cocky, arrogant. Over 1000 goals in his career. No player finished like him.

International Caps	87
World Cup Final Caps	6
World Cup Final Goals	4
Year of Birth	1927

F2	Francisco Gento

As out and out left winger, the fastest thing on two legs and with Di Stefano's passes dominated European football for 5 years. Good finisher too.

International Caps	43
World Cup Final Caps	5
World Cup Final Goals	0
Year of Birth	1933

Real Madrid and the European Cup

The 1950s saw the British game slowly waking up from its aloofness towards the world-wide game. But even after Hungary had embarrassed England at Wembley in 1953 the FA banned Chelsea from entering any European competition.

Spanish giants Real Madrid won the first European Cup, liked the experience and went on to win the next four as well. If the English had thought Madrid's Hungarian star Ferenc Puskas was cutting a portly figure at Wembley, by the late 1950s he was even heavier. His presence alongside the balding Argentinean Alfredo di Stéfano might have lulled opponents into a false sense of security but this rarely lasted as the duo, ably helped by the speedy Gento on the wing, would proceed to blow the opposition away with skill, guile and an avalanche of goals.

The Busby Babes

After English clubs were allowed to compete in the European Cup it was Manchester United that had the most successful early campaigns. Legendary manager Matt Busby assembled a talented young team nicknamed the 'Busby Babes'. On the return journey from a European Cup tie a tragic air crash in Munich claimed the lives of eight members of the squad. The mythology surrounding this tragedy has ensured that cards of the doomed team fetch large premiums.

Colourful Card Sets

Barratt's were often joined in the sweet cigarette card market by numerous short-lived companies. Dickson & Orde of Surrey put out an insightful 50-card set of *Footballers* in 1960 (see overleaf). How many players today can be seen working on their boots with a hammer or pouring a cup of tea in the changing room? The set also showed a couple of young Middlesbrough players – Brian Clough and Peter Taylor – together for the first time.

Barratt's, who had been issuing cards since 1911, began an annual set of football cards in 1952 which continued right until 1967, became erratic for a few years, then appeared annually again between 1977 and 1992.

Above right, Di Stefano (Real Madrid)
Below right, Duncan Edwards (Manchester United)

Top row, left to right:
Gordon Turner (Luton);
Bobby Robson (W.B.A.).

Middle row, left to right:
Wilbur Cush (Leeds);
Brian Clough (Middlesbrough);
Billy Foulkes (Manchester United).

Bottom row, left to right:
Bob Stokoe (Newcastle);
Peter Taylor (Middlesbrough);
Jim Dickinson (Portsmouth).

The 1960s Stickers And All That

Foreign Issues in the Early 1960s

For anyone growing up during the two decades from the mid-1970s onwards, the pinnacle of any football collection had to be a completed Panini album. But the company that became so ingrained into British footballing culture was not just a 1970s phenomenon as it had been formed way back in 1961. Two Italian brothers, Benito and Guiseppe Panini, who owned a newspaper distribution business in Modena, had the idea to produce a collection of cards depicting players from Italy's Serie A. They sold a staggering three million packets of that first series. Today a completed 1961 album can easily fetch over £1,000 at auction.

The business exploded and two more brothers, Franco and Umberto, joined the family firm as it spread to leagues across Europe. The company emblem of a player executing a bicycle kick (taken from a photograph of Juventus' Carlo Parola) rapidly became synonymous with football sticker collecting. From their earliest days the Paninis kept things fresh by including team photos and stadium pictures, as well as covering world and European competitions, and teams and players from the lower leagues.

DANIEL ONEGA

Throughout the early 1960s A & BC were
overindulgent with their early issues. Soon their
football sets were relegated to shorter runs of
black-and-white cards. They did, however, issue a
separate set of Scottish cards each season, which
due to their scarcity regularly fetch double the
price of their English counterparts.

**RON SPRINGETT
SHEFFIELD WEDNESDAY**

No. 39   GOALKEEPER

**ALAN A'COURT
LIVERPOOL**

No. 35   OUTSIDE LEFT

**REG DAVIES
SWANSEA TOWN**

No. 18   OUTSIDE RIGHT

FREDDIE GOODWIN
LEEDS UNITED

No. 21   RIGHT HALF

ROY McCROHAN
NORWICH CITY

No. 45   RIGHT HALF

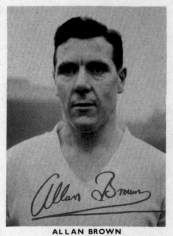

ALLAN BROWN
PORTSMOUTH

No. 30   INSIDE FORWARD

IVOR ALLCHURCH
NEWCASTLE UNITED

No. 47   INSIDE FORWARD

Ted Phillips and Ray Crawford were the
spearhead of Alf Ramsey's exciting Ipswich side
of the early 1960s. After gaining promotion
(with the duo netting over 70 goals between
them) the Tractor Boys swept to the First Division
championship at the first time of asking. Phillips
and Crawford added over 50 more goals
to their personal records.

Tiger Star Footballers of 1963, opposite,
clockwise from top left:
Alex Elder (Burnley);
Gordon Banks (Leicester City);
Peter Swan (Sheffield Wednesday);
Ray Parry (Blackpool)

Page 60, clockwise from top left:
Colin Appleton (Leicester City);
Joe Baker (Arsenal);
Danny Blanchflower (Tottenham Hotspur);
Alex Hamilton (Dundee)

Page 61, clockwise from top left:
Bobby Moore (West Ham United);
Johnny Byrne (West Ham United);
Roger Hunt (Liverpool);
Derek Tapscott (Cardiff City)

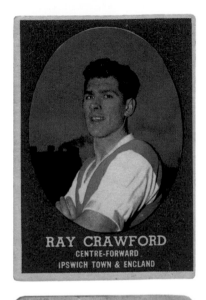

RAY CRAWFORD
CENTRE-FORWARD
IPSWICH TOWN & ENGLAND

TED
PHILLIPS
INSIDE-LEFT

52

TED
PHILLIPS

TED'S THUNDERBOLT
SHOOTING – TIMED
AT 67. M.P.H. MEANS
HE NEEDS VERY
CLOSE MARKING

PRINTED IN ENGLAND

★ Bazooka ★
THE CHEW OF CHAMPIONS

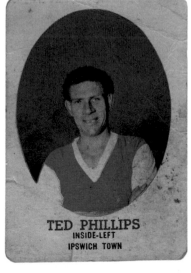

TED PHILLIPS
INSIDE-LEFT
IPSWICH TOWN

A & BC returned to full colour and stylish designs in the 1963–64 season. Unfortunately, though, the photo quality left something to be desired.

TONY
HATELEY
Centre Forward
Notts County

JOHN
BARNWELL
Right Half
Arsenal

MOORE

DEREK
DOUGAN
Centre Forward
Aston Villa & N. Ireland

RONNIE
REES
Outside Left
Coventry City

BILLY
BREMNER
Inside Forward
United

GORDON
BANKS
Goalkeeper
Leicester City & England

ALBERT McCANN
Portsmouth F.C.   Inside Left

JOHN McSEVENEY
Hull City F.C.   Outside Left

TERRY VENABLES
Chelsea F.C.   Inside Right

JOHN NEWMAN
Plymouth Argyle F.C.   Left Half

BARRY LINES
Northampton Town F.C.   Outside Left

NOEL DWYER
Swansea Town F.C.   Goalkeeper
Eire

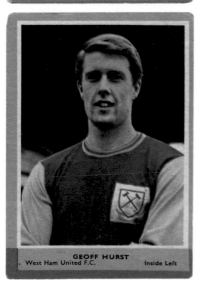

GEOFF HURST
. West Ham United F.C.   Inside Left

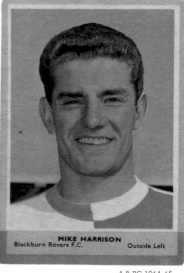

MIKE HARRISON
Blackburn Rovers F.C.   Outside Left

A & BC 1964–65

World Cup 1966

Of course, this was the pinnacle of English football: 1966 and all that; 'They think it's all over'; the Russian (*sic*: he was actually from Azerbaijan) linesman; Nobby Stiles' missing front teeth; Bobby Moore being carried around Wembley with Jules Rimet still gleaming. The tournament predictably spawned a massive interest in English football, from which the world of cards and stickers benefited greatly. But there were surprisingly few cards about the World Cup itself. A couple of overseas companies produced sticker albums in the run-up to the competition, but aside from that it was pretty much business as usual. A & BC did use a photograph of the victorious English line-up as a multi-card checklist for their 1966–67 season cards, and Alf Ramsey was included in Brooke Bond tea's *Famous People* series; but it was left to the losing Germans to produce a stamp-like set that gave their conquerors the credit they truly deserved.

Geoffrey Hurst

Jack Charlton

Post-1966 Explosion

Eventually, though, as the significance of England's 1966 win began to sink in, the marketing men's minds set to work on how they could cash in. Newspapers began giving more coverage to football, new magazines appeared, games and toys were selling like hot cakes and card issues grew in number.

The Lisbon Lions

Scottish footballers have always been seen as the poor relations of their English counterparts as far as cards and stickers are concerned. Whether it's the smaller league or lower average attendances, the teams north of the border often get a raw deal. Few sticker albums have concentrated on Scottish football, and in most years the Scottish section of the Panini album featured half-sized Scottish players so two could fit on one sticker and save space at the back of the book. As with A & BC's Scottish cards, though, Panini's Scots are now highly collectable (and therefore expensive).

Unsurprisingly, Rangers and Celtic cards are most in demand. And top of everyone's list is a team card of Celtic's European Cup winners from 1967. For the sake of my marriage, I hope my wife doesn't read this book in detail, because collecting Lisbon Lions cards is a passion of mine. A recent eBay lot of Celtic A & BC beauties reached over £100, but to make up for my frivolity I was able to sell the doubles from the set for over £10 each.

This page: John Hughes (top); Billy McNeill. Opposite page, clockwise from top left: Tommy Gemmell; Jimmy Johnstone; Bobby Lennox; Bertie Auld.

GOALKEEPER
PETER SHILTON
LEICESTER C.

GOALKEEPER
GORDON BANKS
STOKE C.

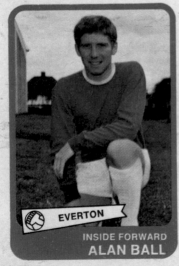

INSIDE FORWARD
ALAN BALL
EVERTON

INSIDE LEFT
RODNEY MARSH
Q.P.R.

WEST HAM U.

C. FORWARD
GEOFF HURST

WEST HAM U.

L. HALF
BOBBY MOORE

SUNDERLAND

GOALKEEPER
JIM MONTGOMERY

SHEFFIELD W.

INSIDE RIGHT
JIM McCALLIOG

A & BC 1967–68

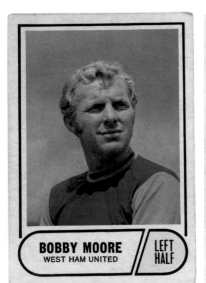

BOBBY MOORE
WEST HAM UNITED

LEFT HALF

DENIS LAW
MANCHESTER UNITED

INSIDE LEFT

GORDON BANKS
STOKE CITY

GOAL KEEPER

FRED KEMP
SOUTHAMPTON

RIGHT HALF

ROGER MORGAN
TOTTENHAM HOTSPUR
OUTSIDE LEFT

JEFF ASTLE
WEST BROMWICH ALBION
CENTRE FORWARD

NEIL YOUNG
MANCHESTER CITY
INSIDE LEFT

WILF SMITH
SHEFFIELD WEDNESDAY
RIGHT BACK

A & BC 1969–70

FKS in the UK

The late 1960s saw a new development in the UK – the football sticker. Panini had been issuing small cards that could be stuck into albums for a few years, and now the gradual change to stickers was evolving. Initially these were little more than flimsy pieces of paper that required glue to stick them into their albums. Later, they came with peelable backs.

Over the next decade the competition between cards proper and stickers reach its peak. As well as trading stickers, boys up and down the country spent hours in the school yard playing games to win more cards for their sets. Then at the weekend all their pocket money was spent on new packs of cards. Would that elusive Charlie George or Bobby Moore sticker be inside? No, it was always another Leicester City or Sunderland player!

FKS arrived on the scene in the late 1960s to dazzle schoolboys with a colourful series of 330 stickers under the thrilling title of *The Wonderful World of Soccer Stars*. What made things even more exciting was the availability of an album to keep them all in for just 3s 6d. There were some drawbacks, however. These were a long way from the slick 1970s stickers that had peel-off backs and were ready to stick straight into your album. The FKS issues were plain-backed and had to be glued in place. And this was before Pritt Stick was around to make the gluing process simple.

Though the albums were produced in England, the stickers were printed in Spain to minimise cost. More money seems to have been saved by not employing a proof-reader: a complete album would be full of mistakes, misspelt names and the like. In spite of the cost-cutting, though, this first FKS set is now highly collectable, and stickers that have never been stuck can fetch a couple of pounds each. The 330 stickers in the first set consisted of 15 for each of the 22 First Division sides, with no text or information about the players in the album. The following year this was addressed, with a short biography of each player being provided, though in many cases the same photograph was used for 1968–69 as had appeared in 1967–68.

FKS would continue to produce colourful sets into the 1980s. While they kept them plain and simple in the early days, they started to experiment with multiple images and overly fussy artwork in the mid-1970s. Nevertheless, hard as they tried, they would always seem to be Panini's poorer cousin.

Opposite page, clockwise from top left:
Jackie Sinclair (Newcastle United); Jackie Charlton (Leeds United); Dietmar Bruck (Coventry City); Allan Clarke (Leicester City).

Page 76, clockwise from top left: Marvin Hinton (Chelsea); Mick Mills (Ipswich Town); Mel Blyth (Crystal Palace); Steve Kember (Crystal Palace)

Page 77, clockwise from top left:
Willie Carr (Coventry City); Peter Eustace (Sheffield Wednesday); Pat Jennings (Tottenham Hotspur); Les Latcham (Burnley)

SERIE **A** ROMA

SERGIO SANTARINI

SERIE **A** FIORENTINA

CLAUDIO MERLO

SERIE **A** NAPOLI

ANTONIO JULIANO

SERIE **A** VERONA

SERGIO MADDE'

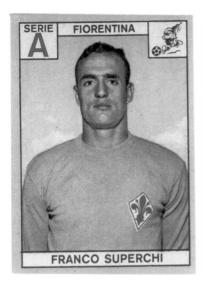

SERIE A · FIORENTINA

FRANCO SUPERCHI

SERIE A · PALERMO

GIANVITO GEOTTI

SERIE A · PISA

SANDRO JOAN

SERIE A · PALERMO

MARIO GIUBERTONI

Panini, Serie A 1968–69

The 1970s

Breakfast Cereal and Other Issues

Cards and stickers were now well established as accompaniments to a wide range of commodities. Shredded Wheat breakfast cereal issued a series of football stickers in sets of three and Typhoo Tea was renowned as the football fan's drink of choice. The latter issued cards to be cut out from their tea packets between 1963 and 1973. Like other cards that required cutting out, those that are available today vary greatly in quality, so prices differ wildly.

Once a certain amount of packets (usually 12) had been collected you could send off for a sturdy 10 x 8 inch colour photo of a favourite player or team group.

QPR full-back Jimmy Langley was an avid collector and was featured in *Goal* magazine with his 100,000 cards, then valued at a total of £500. He explained that Johnny Haynes' parents had given him over fifty sets of cards from packets of tea. 'They must drink a lot of tea in the Haynes household,' he quipped.

Picture No. 29

Jackie Charlton, iron-man for Leeds and England

MOISTEN THIS SIDE TO STICK

Petrol Collections

In the early 1970s petrol companies began giving out football memorabilia when you filled up your tank. The famous Esso 1970 World Cup coin collection is fondly remembered, and the Cleveland chain of pumping stations weighed in with their Jimmy Hill- and Brian Moore-endorsed *Golden Goals* sticker collection. When spending a pound or buying more than three gallons of petrol you received a large envelope which contained between one and three stickers. For just 20 pence you could then buy a stylish hard-backed album in which to stick your collection.

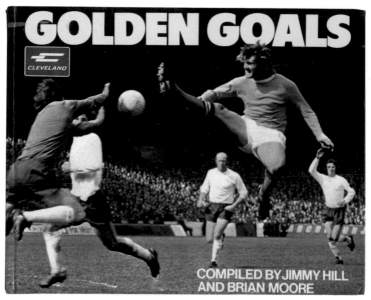

COMPILED BY JIMMY HILL AND BRIAN MOORE

World Cup 1970

While the 1966 World Cup was England's greatest footballing moment, the 1970 tournament has become the most mythologised. It was the first time that England went abroad with a realistic chance of winning; Banks and Pelé duelled; but ultimately the best team of all time, the Brazil of Carlos Alberto, Jairzinho and Rivelino (as well as Pelé), strolled to victory in the Azteca.

Mexico 1970 has become a cornerstone of football collecting. I have occasionally succumbed to what many other online auction bidders have put themselves through: the early morning alarm. This is usually the fault of uncaring North American sellers whose auctions end around 3.46 am UK time. So the alarm is set, the computer booted up while eyes are rubbed, and then last-minute bids are made. If successful, you can return to bed safe in the knowledge that you've just got the last five Honduras players you need at a bargain price, even after postage.

Both FKS and Panini produced UK sticker collections for the tournament. The contrast couldn't have been greater between the two sets, but both are highly collectable and charming in their own ways. It was with this set that FKS started to use artwork of a Brazilian player executing an overhead kick as the cover for their album, and they would continue to do so for the World Cups of 1974, 1978 and 1982.

ENGLAND   1970

MEXICO 70

CAMPEONATO MUNDIAL
DE FUTBOL

All players and teams participating
and THE HISTORY of the
WORLD CUP
Ask your retailer for the album for
collecting the cards.

Tous les joueurs, les équipes partici-
pants et l'HISTOIRE des
CHAMPIONNATS DU MONDE
Demandez chez votre détaillant l'album pour la collection des vignettes.

Alle Spieler, Mannschaften und
GESCHICHTE der
FUSSBALLWELTMEISTERSCHAFT
Unsere Album für die Bildersammlung
sind bei Ihrem Verkäufer verfügbar.

PRINTED IN ITALY BY
EDIZIONI PANINI - MODENA ©

BRASIL

DIRCEU LOPES

MEXICO 70

19 70

BRASIL

EDÚ

MEXICO 70

19 70

BRASIL

CARLOS ALBERTO

MEXICO 70

19 70

BRASIL

GERSON

MEXICO 70

19 70

World Cup 1970 Panini

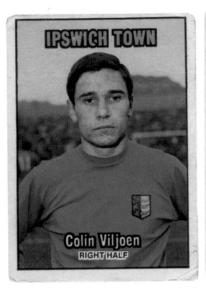

IPSWICH TOWN

Colin Viljoen
RIGHT HALF

WEST HAM UNITED

Clyde Best
INSIDE FORWARD

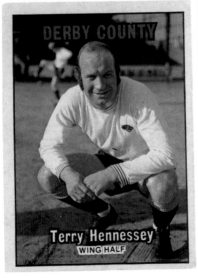

DERBY COUNTY

Terry Hennessey
WING HALF

MANCHESTER CITY

Francis Lee
CENTRE FORWARD

SOUTHAMPTON

Mike Channon
INSIDE LEFT

WEST HAM UNITED

Harry Redknapp
OUTSIDE LEFT

COVENTRY CITY

Neil Martin
CENTRE FORWARD

COVENTRY CITY

Willie Carr
INSIDE RIGHT

A & BC 1970-71

CRYSTAL PALACE

STEVE KEMBER
INSIDE FORWARD

WEST HAM UNITED

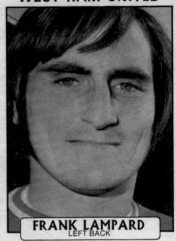

FRANK LAMPARD
LEFT BACK

HUDDERSFIELD TOWN

JIMMY NICHOLSON
WING HALF

NEWCASTLE UNITED

FRANK CLARK
LEFT BACK

STOKE CITY

JIMMY GREENHOFF
CENTRE FORWARD

ARSENAL

CHARLIE GEORGE
INSIDE FORWARD

DUNDEE

JIM STEELE
WING HALF

WEST BROMWICH ALBION

ASA HARTFORD
INSIDE FORWARD

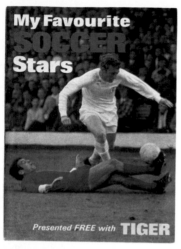

IPC Boys' Comics

IPC will forever be in the football fan's heart as being the publisher of the much-loved *Shoot!* magazine. But it was a number of other comics and magazines from their stable that provided early 1970s collectors with a host of cards and albums. *Buster*, *Lion*, *Scorcher*, *Smash* and *Tiger* all gave away sets of eight cards a week for four weeks under the banner *My Favourite Soccer Stars*. These would then be mounted in mini-albums that were also given away by the comics. The drawback was that you had to buy all five magazines each week for a month in order to collect the full 160 cards that were issued; something that would have been financially challenging for any young collector.

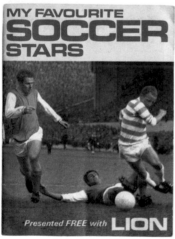

Another periodical collection came from Marshall Cavendish's *Book of Football*. This was a 75-week part work that built into a five-volume football encyclopedia. Unusually, some issues also came with a sheet of 16 colour pictures to be cut out and stuck in the *Book of Football* album. For some reason, 44 pictures were pre-printed in the album, leaving you to collect another 320 over 20 weeks.

J. Radford *(Arsenal)*

R. Davies *(Southampton)*

R. Barron *(Northampton)*

G. Reece *(Sheff. Utd.)*

G. Young *(Sheff. Wed.)*

P. Dobing *(Stoke City)*

E. Hunt *(Coventry)*

B. Jones *(Cardiff)*

N. Hunter *(Leeds)*

M. England *(Spurs)*

R. Hunt *(Liverpool)*

B. Bridges *(Q.P.R.)*

The Tabloids

Never an industry to miss a good marketing opportunity, the tabloid press started to use football cards as a marketing gimmick at the start of the 1970s. The *Sun* printed tokens every day during the 1970–71 season which could be redeemed for their 134-card *Football Swap Card* series. The following season they experimented with their *Soccerstamps*. In 1972 they turned to issuing 3D cards. Some larger cards featured a posed portrait shot of a player, while smaller ones gave the impression of a moving image when tilted back and forth. These usually showed a player heading, dribbling or kicking on the training ground.

IAN STOREY-MOORE
Notts Forest
186

Not to be left out, the *Daily Mirror* issued its *Star Soccer Sides* in the 1971–72 season. These smallish cards featured team pictures of all 92 Football League clubs plus the four Home International teams. You could also send off for larger cards of your favourite club. It was a nice set because clubs of all sizes were included equally.

ALAN CAMPBELL
Charlton Athletic
119

JOHN O'HARE
Derby County
97

PETER OSGOOD
Chelsea
94

MALCOLM MacDONALD
Luton Town
122

JIMMY GREAVES
West Ham
111

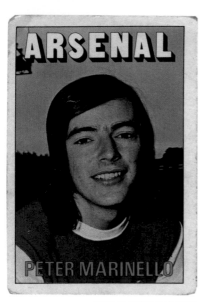

ARSENAL

PETER MARINELLO

LEICESTER

MID-FIELD

DAVID NISH

MANCHESTER C.

BACK-FOUR

WILLIE DONACHIE

TOTTENHAM

FULL-BACK

JOE KINNEAR

SHEFFIELD U.

TONY CURRIE

MID-FIELD

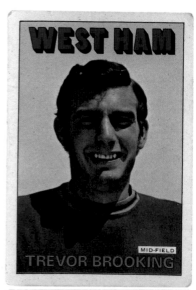

WEST HAM

TREVOR BROOKING

MID-FIELD

ARSENAL

BOB WILSON

GOALKEEPER

CRYSTAL PALACE

MEL BLYTH

BACK-FOUR

A & BC 1972-73

IPSWICH TOWN

ALLAN HUNTER

NORWICH

GRAHAM PADDON

BIRMINGHAM

GORDON TAYLOR

LEEDS UTD.

ALLAN CLARKE

CHELSEA

PETER OSGOOD

LIVERPOOL

KEVIN KEEGAN

EVERTON

DAVE LAWSON

LEICESTER

DENNIS ROFE

A & BC 1973-74

Top Sellers, effectively a franchise of Panini, produced several albums which are extremely hard to find. They sell for hundreds of pounds when they do come up for sale.

Clockwise from top left:
Peter Wall (Crystal Palace); Ian St. John (Coventry City); Ian Britton (Chelsea); John McGovern (Derby County); Greame Souness (Middlesbrough); John Tudor (Newcastle United)

Flicking Games

Like many things that make their way into the hands of children, a card's value soon drops with a little bit of wear and tear. The usual practice of securing a stack of cards with an elastic band wasn't enough. The games that were dreamt up so you could gamble and win or lose your prize assets have ruined many a good collection.

Deviations on Snap weren't too destructive, but 'flicking games' caused carnage. Many variations were thought up, and some of the most popular are listed here.

1. Two or more players line up a set distance from a wall and flick their chosen card towards it. The person who gets their card closest to the wall without touching it wins all the cards.

2. As above, but the players have to make the card bounce off the wall. The furthest from the wall wins all the cards.

3. In a two-player game turns are taken to flick a card and the first person to get one of their cards to land on their opponent's wins all the cards.

4. Each player lines up a set amount of cards at an angle against the base of a wall. Players then take turns flicking cards to try to knock down the cards. The player who overturns the last standing card wins the lot.

FKS in the 1970s

Unlike Panini, FKS initially concentrated solely on the English First Division. The 20-pence albums usually held 14 or 15 players per team, and to make life difficult the text about each player was written in the rectangle where the sticker would be housed. You therefore had to glue a small sliver across the top of the sticker so that it could be lifted to allow reading.

FKS were at pains to point out the virtues of the collection, and printed the following in the back of the album: 'The publishers unreservedly warrant that an identical quantity of stamps of every number and letter have been printed. No specific stamps have been withheld or kept in short supply in the special mixing process.' They also rather curiously stated, 'In order to maintain authenticity, some of the players have been photographed in clothing which is not necessarily their official club colours.'

Apply adhesive here only.

- -

1

ARSENAL

(A full biography on this player will be found in the appropriate space in the album).

The Most Expensive Sticker Albums

Complete and in Very Good or better condition

Manufacturer	Series (year of issue)	Price
Top Sellers	Football 72 (1972)	£200.00
Top Sellers	Football 73 (1973)	£175.00
Top Sellers	Football 74 (1974)	£125.00
Ava Americana	Football Special (1978)	£100.00
Panini	Mexico 70 (1970)	£100.00
Panini	Football Clubs (1975)	£100.00
Top Sellers	Football 75 (1975)	£100.00
FKS	Euro Stars (1977)	£90.00
Panini	München 74 (1974)	£90.00
FKS	Soccer Stars (1977)	£90.00
FKS	Soccer Stars (1968)	£85.00
Panini	Euro Football 78 (1978)	£80.00
FKS	Argentina 78 (1978)	£75.00
FKS	Mexico 70 (1970)	£75.00
Panini	Euro Football 79 (1979)	£75.00

THE WONDERFUL WORLD OF
SOCCER STARS
1974/75

20p

ARSENAL

Founded: 1886; Ground:
Highbury; Manager: Bertie
Mee; League Champions:
1931, 1933, 1934, 1935, 1938,
1948, 1953, 1971; F.A. Cup:
1930, 1936, 1950, 1971; Fairs
Cup: 1970

GEORGE ARMSTRONG

ALAN BALL

JEFF BLOCKLEY

CHARLIE GEORGE

EDDIE KELLY

RAY KENNEDY

BOB McNAB

SAMMY NELSON

DAVID PRICE

JOHN RADFORD

PAT RICE

JIMMY RIMMER

PETER SIMPSON

PETER STOREY

CARLISLE UNITED

Founded: 1904; Ground:
Brunton Park; Manager:
Alan Ashman.

CHRIS BALDERSTONE

PETER CARR

FRANK CLARKE

TOM CLARKE

JOHN GORMAN

BILL GREEN

JOE LAIDLAW

DENNIS MARTIN

LES O'NEILL

BOBBY OWEN

ALLAN ROSS

STAN TERNENT

MIKE McCARTNEY

RAY TRAIN

GRAHAM WINSTANLEY

LEEDS UNITED

Founded: 1920; Ground:
Elland Road; Manager: Don
Revie; League Champions:
1969, 1974; F.A. Cup: 1972;
League Cup: 1968; Fairs
Cup: 1968, 1971

MICK BATES

BILLY BREMNER

TREVOR CHERRY

ALLAN CLARKE

JOHNNY GILES

EDDIE GRAY

DAVID HARVEY

NORMAN HUNTER

MICK JONES

JOE JORDAN

PETER LORIMER

GORDON McQUEEN

PAUL MADELEY

PAUL REANEY

TERRY YORATH

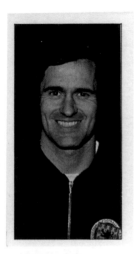

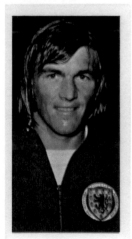

Topps

Topps had been a well-known US baseball, ice-hockey, basketball and gridiron card producer since 1938. But by the mid-1970s they were looking to expand into Europe.

In 1974 they saw their perfect opportunity in the ailing A & BC Company. Over the next six seasons they introduced the *Shoot!*, *Goal!*, *All-stars* and *Great Britain Select Eleven* sub-sets. In 1978 they produced the Scottish sub-set of *World Cup All-Stars*, but by the time you'd collected all of them the 'stars' were already on their way home from Argentina.

Topps' legacy is one of colourful cards with design in keeping with the times: they were produced in the garish glam-rock-inspired tones of the mid-1970s. Today all of the Topps sets are very collectable, though the sticks of chemically flavoured bubblegum that accompanied them are not!

Apart from beating Zaire and exiting the tournament unbeaten, Scotland's only other highlight from the World Cup was to feature heavily in this moody Germany '74 set of cards.

Opposite page clockwise from top left: George Graham; Franz Beckenbauer; Denis Law; Sandy Jardine; Johnny Repp; Kenny Dalglish

IPSWICH

GEORGE BURLEY

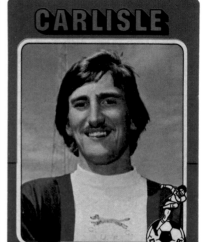

CARLISLE

BILL GREEN

SUNDERLAND

BOBBY MONCUR

DUNDEE UNITED

GEORGE FLEMING

CARLISLE

RAY TRAIN

MIDFIELD

DUNDEE

JOCKY SCOTT

MIDFIELD

LUTON TOWN

ALAN WEST

MIDFIELD

ARSENAL

GEORGE ARMSTRONG

FORWARD

Topps 1974–75

Hints and Tips

As times change, so do the hints and tips that are offered on the cards. Even back with John Player's *Hints on Association Football* in 1929 one card lamented, 'The shoulder charge is not used as much today as formerly.' It wasn't all just kick-and-rush and blood-and-thunder in the old days, though, as more subtle – some might say showboating – hints were also provided. In the 1950s the *Hotspur* 'paper for boys' gave away one card that talked you through how to score with a back-heel from inside the six-yard box.

Another popular collection was tea producer Brooke Bond's *Play Better Soccer*, which perhaps misguidedly gave tips from the hapless mid-1970s England squad. Gerry Francis, Mike Channon, Colin Todd and Ray Clemence shared their knowledge on the 'banana shot', 'cutting inside', 'the back-heel' and 'diving' – which in those more innocent times was demonstrated by Clemence, not one of the forwards!

USE YOUR HEAD AND WING IT .

Oh, the excitement. To rip open a packet and see a club badge peeping out of the enclosed stickers. The experimental cloth variety (below) were used by Panini for only one season: 1979–80. Even today, middle-aged collectors are happy to pay silly money for these.

How We Used to Collect

This author was surely not the only child of the 1970s to buy *Shoot!* magazine for the free album and packet of six stickers before morosely realising that to complete the set I would need another 594! Despite this seemingly insurmountable task, I would dash off to the newsagent's with my weekly 35 pence pocket money to buy seven packets at 5 pence each. Of course, come the end of the season, the half-filled album would be stuffed into the back of a drawer, but by August the new season's collection would be started with undiminished vigour.

In the 1970s it was really something to be able to 'own' a piece of your hero, even if it was 'just' a picture on a card. You took them everywhere in school-blazer pockets and stuffed into satchels, ready for a swap or a game at a moment's notice.

Throughout the 1960s and 1970s we really became a nation of collectors. Items from this era are now the centrepieces of retro-chic TV programmes like *Twentieth Century Roadshow*. But back then we had just three TV channels, Action Man, Airfix models and football cards. There was no Pokémon, no PlayStations, no *Star Wars*, no Premiership on Sky. Owning the cards really meant something. We were happy to spend hours simply reading and re-reading the cards and albums. By the end of the season, they were often memorised.

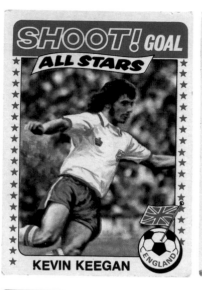

KEVIN KEEGAN

PETER SHILTON

SAMMY McILROY

RAY CLEMENCE

PARTICK THISTLE

ALAN ROUGH

Q.P.R.

PHIL PARKES

The Panini Album

The Panini album has become an iconic image in football memorabilia, if not in twentieth-century design as a whole. After the memorable World Cup and European albums, they took over from Top Sellers and issued the *Football 78* album, which started a run of 18 consecutive sticker albums that ended with Euro '96.

The usual form was to have two pages for each of the 22 First Division clubs, including the manager, a team picture and a special badge, usually printed on gold or silver foil but sometimes on cloth. Die-hards would spend ages ensuring they lined up each sticker perfectly inside the pre-printed boxes in the album. Second Division teams usually had just a team photo and a badge to collect, while Third Division teams had the team photo and mini-badge. If you were unlucky enough to support a Fourth Division team, you were ignored altogether. So relegation in those days was a double whammy: a real-life drop also meant demotion (or even extermination) in the sticker-collecting stakes.

Grids of fixtures for each division were included so you could religiously fill in every score at Saturday teatime. To keep things fresh, each year also saw a selection of themed stickers to collect: European games, famous FA Cup finals, award-winners or

30/1/82(5)/6/2/82(7)/18/2/82(10)/3/3/82(14)/

LIVERPOOL

FIRST DIVISION

First Division

LIVERPOOL

Chairman: J W Smith, J.P.

Manager: Bob Paisley

Secretary: P B Robinson

Coach: Ron Moran

Captain: Phil Thompson

Year formed: 1892

Ground capacity: 52,518

Record attendance: 61,905 v Wolves, F.A. Cup, 4th Rd, Feb. 2, 1952.

Football League record: Div. One: 1894-95, 1896-1904, 1905-54, 1962- , Div. Two: 1893-94, 1895-96, 1904-05, 1954-62.

Honours: Div. One Champions: 1900-01, 1905-06, 1921-22, 1922-23, 1946-47, 1963-64, 1965-66, 1972-73, 1975-76, 1976-77, 1978-79, 1979-80. These 12 victories constitute a record. Div. Two Champions: 1893-94, 1895-96, 1904-05, 1961-62. F.A. Cup winners: 1965, 1974. League Cup winners: 1981. European Cup winners: 1977, 1978, 1981. U.E.F.A. Cup winners: 1973, 1976.

Colours: All red with white trim.

Change colours: White shirts with red collars and cuffs, black shorts, white stockings.

BRUCE GROBBELAAR
LIVERPOOL

PHIL NEAL
LIVERPOOL

ALAN HANSEN
LIVERPOOL

MARK LAWRENSON
LIVERPOOL

PHIL THOMPSON
LIVERPOOL

CRAIG JOHNSTON
LIVERPOOL

BRUCE GROBBELAAR Goalkeeper. Born Zimbabwe. Ht. 6.0 Wt. 12.0 Age 24. A Zimbabwe international goalkeeper who made his League debut as a non-contract player for Crewe Alexandra against Wigan in December 1979, going on to make 24 League appearances and score one goal (a penalty) before joining Vancouver Whitecaps in the N.A.S.L. Cost Liverpool the sum of £250,000 when they bought him from Vancouver, and he will be the replacement for Ray Clemence in 1981-82.

PHIL NEAL Defender. Born Irchester. Ht. 5.11 Wt. 12.2 Age 30. Incredibly, Phil Neal has not missed a single League game for Liverpool during the past six seasons. Made his League debut with Northampton Town in 1968, and was transferred to Liverpool for a more £65,000 in October 1974. Now has well over 550 first team games behind him, and has been a fairly regular member of the England side in recent years. Gets his name on the scoresheet occasionally. ■ 32 □ 3 (E)

ALAN HANSEN Defender. Born Alloa. Ht. 6.1 Wt. 13.0 Age 26. A former Scottish Under-23 and Under-21 player who has established himself in the centre of the Liverpool defence in place of Emlyn Hughes. Started his career with Partick Thistle joining the Anfield staff in May 1977 in a £100,000 transfer. His first season with the club was rounded off by an appearance in the European Cup final, and he is also a regular member of the Scotland squad. ■ 7 □ 0 (S)

MARK LAWRENSON Defender. Born Preston. Ht. 5.11 Wt. 11.6 Age 25. Started his career as a defender with Preston, but after moving to Brighton for £100,000 in June 1977 he operated successfully in midfield or defence, and had also started to establish himself as an Eire international. Liverpool signed him for the huge fee of £900,000 in August 1981, and no doubt he will be a regular member of the first team in season 1981-82, mostly in defence. ■ 14 □ 1 (EI)

PHIL THOMPSON Defender. Born Liverpool. Ht. 6.0 Wt. 11.8 Age 27. A former England Under-23 player who joined Liverpool as an apprentice in January 1971 and made his League debut against Manchester United in April 1972. Has made nearly 300 League appearances for Liverpool since then, and although formerly a midfield player, he is now recognised as one of the finest central defenders in the game. His 1980-81 appearances were restricted by a troublesome injury. ■ 29 □ 0 (E)

CRAIG JOHNSTON Midfield. Born Johannesburg. Ht. 5.9 Wt. 11.2 Age 23. Although born in Johannesburg, he spent most of his childhood in Australia, and when Middlesbrough toured there in 1975 he was so impressed that he made the trip to England and signed up at Ayresome Park. Made his League debut against Birmingham in Feburary 1978, and went on to clock up 64 League games for Boro before transferring to Liverpool in April 1981.

18

top goal-scorers. Then, on the inside back page, was possibly the most important section of the whole album: the instructions on how you could order the last few stickers to complete your set. For the princely sum of 3 pence per sticker you could send off for any 50 of the elusive stickers. Whether it was that pesky Stoke City team picture or the St Johnstone manager, you could be saved from the niggling acceptance that you had *almost* finished the book.

1970s Panini Euro Series

After replacing Top Sellers, Panini eased into the British market through its four-yearly World Cup albums and a number of Euro albums. The latter were normally a seemingly random selection of European players from club sides. The stickers were slightly smaller than the usual Panini sets but displayed colourful, unfamiliar team strips and club badges. More often than not, the teams were unpronounceable to a young British fan, but when the location of the club's home country was in doubt, at least the ever-helpful folks at Panini provided a map.

GRZEGORZ LATO
POLSKA

RUUD KROL
NEDERLAND

CESKOSLOVENSKO

DUKLA

PRAHA

SPARTA

SLOVAN

Bratislava

INTERNACIONAL

SLAVIA

BANIK

Ostrava

Trnava

SPARTAK

GERD MÜLLER
DEUTSCHLAND - BRD

MARIAN MASNY
CESKOSLOVENSKO

Other Sticker Albums

By the late 1970s Panini had set the standards by which all other sticker albums would be measured. FKS was reaching the end of its natural life, so it was the mysterious – but ultimately patchy – Ava Americana that emerged to challenge the Italian giants. Their *Football Special* sets of 1978 and 1979 left a lot to be desired, even though they secured the endorsement of Arsenal striker Malcolm MacDonald. In his introduction to *Football Special 79* he claimed that the album would be filled with 'hundreds of superb colour pictures'. This claim wasn't totally true, but at least it was a big improvement on their effort of the previous year. That album had featured numerous mistakes and poor-quality photos that had seemingly been assembled from several seasons' worth of pictures: players from the same team were often pictured wearing several different versions of their club's strip. Even worse, the Nottingham Forest team had Peter Shilton in his Stoke City shirt, while David Needham's and Archie Gemmill's heads had obviously been transplanted on to other players' bodies!

NOTTINGHAM FOREST

GROUND: City Ground CAPACITY: 40,000 NICKNAME: The Reds YEAR FORMED: 1865

Honours

Division 1 Champions:
1977-78
Division 2 Champions:
1906-07 1921-22
Division 3 Champions:
1950-51
FA Cup Winners:
1897-98 1958-59
Football League Cup Winners:
1977-78

247
KENNY BURNS

VIV ANDERSON

DAVE NEEDHAM

CLUB COLOURS
SHIRTS: Red.
SHORTS: White.
STOCKINGS: Red.

JOHN McGOVERN

PETER SHILTON

COLIN BARRETT

FRANK CLARK

PETER WITHE

ARCHIE GEMMILL

252
MARTIN O'NEILL

TONY WOODCOCK

IAN BOWYER

253
JOHN ROBERTSON

LARRY LLOYD

79

Season	Div.	Pos.	P.	W.	D.	L.	F.	A.	Pts.
1968-69	1	18	42	10	13	19	45	57	33
1969-70	1	15	42	10	18	14	50	71	38
1970-71	1	16	42	14	8	20	42	61	36
1971-72	1	21	42	8	9	25	47	81	25
1972-73	2	14	42	14	10	18	47	52	40
1973-74	2	7	42	15	15	12	49	42	45
1974-75	2	16	42	12	14	16	43	55	38
1975-76	2	8	42	17	12	13	55	40	46
1976-77	2	3	42	21	10	11	77	43	52
1977-78	1	1	42	25	14	3	69	24	64

10 year stat's

FOREST

MANCHESTER CITY

GROUND: Maine Road CAPACITY: 52,500 NICKNAME: The Citizens YEAR FORMED: 1887

Honours

Division 1 Champions:
1936-37 1967-68
Division 2 Champions:
1898-99 1902-03 1909-10 1927-28
1946-47 1965-66
FA Cup Winners:
1903-04 1933-34 1955-56 1968-69
Football League Cup Winners:
1969-70 1975-76
European Cup Winners Cup:
1969-70

PETER BARNES

MIKE CHANNON

ASA HARTFORD

CLUB COLOURS
SHIRTS: Sky blue with collar and cuffs.
SHORTS: Sky blue with white trimmings.
STOCKINGS: Sky blue with white trips.

DAVE WATSON

JOE CORRIGAN

COLIN BELL

KEN CLEMENTS

GARY OWEN

GERRY KEEGAN

WILLIE DONACHIE

PAUL POWER

TOMMY BOOTH

BRIAN KIDD

MIKE DOYLE

79

Season	Div.	Pos.	P.	W.	D.	L.	F.	A.	Pts.
1968-69	1	13	42	15	10	17	64	55	40
1969-70	1	10	42	16	11	15	55	48	43
1970-71	1	11	42	12	17	13	47	42	41
1971-72	1	4	42	23	11	8	77	45	57
1972-73	1	11	42	15	11	16	57	60	41
1973-74	1	14	42	14	12	16	39	46	40
1974-75	1	8	42	18	10	14	54	54	46
1975-76	1	8	42	19	11	12	64	48	43
1976-77	1	2	42	21	14	7	60	34	56
1977-78	1	4	42	20	12	10	74	51	52

10 year stat's

It's often the disposable items from everyday life that end up being the most collectable. A perfect example is the football sticker packet. Millions of these must have been bought and thrown away over the years, but now they sell for several pounds each, and in some cases much more than that. They also conjure up some of the strongest memories of childhood.

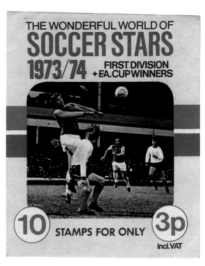

THE WONDERFUL WORLD OF
SOCCER STARS
1973/74 FIRST DIVISION + F.A. CUP WINNERS

10 STAMPS FOR ONLY 3p incl. VAT

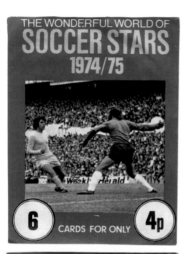

THE WONDERFUL WORLD OF
SOCCER STARS
1974/75

6 CARDS FOR ONLY 4p

This packet contains 6 cards in brilliant colour from the collection
THE WONDERFUL WORLD OF
SOCCER STARS
1974/75

Published by
F.K.S. Publishers Ltd,
Warwick House
334 Kilburn High Road,
London NW6 2QN

PRINTED IN SPAIN

This packet contains 10 stamps in brilliant colour from the collection
THE WONDERFUL WORLD OF
SOCCER STARS
1973/74
FIRST DIVISION + F.A. CUP WINNERS

Published by:
F.K.S. Publishers Ltd.,
F.K.S. House, 175 Wardour St.,
London W.1.

PRINTED IN SPAIN

SOCCER STARS 80

FIVE SELF-ADHESIVE STICKERS   5p

COLLECTORS ALBUM
AVAILABLE FROM YOUR
LOCAL NEWSAGENT

 F.K.S. Publishers Ltd.,
Warwick House, 334 Kilburn
High Road, London NW6 2QN

COLLECTORS ALBUM
AVAILABLE FROM YOUR
LOCAL NEWSAGENT

PRINTED IN SPAIN

 F.K.S. Publishers Ltd.,
Warwick House, 334 Kilburn
High Road, London NW6 2QN

FOOTBALL 78

5p.

FIGURINE PANINI

MOST CAPS
TERRY COOPER
(ENGLAND) 20

LEAGUE GOALS
JOHN HICKTON
159

MIDDLESBROUGH
TEAM LEADERS

LEA. APPEARANCES
JOHN HICKTON 393

BIG FEE MAN
PHIL BOERSMA £75,000

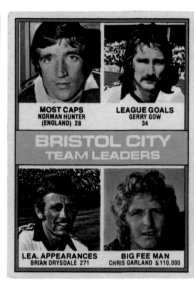

MOST CAPS
NORMAN HUNTER
(ENGLAND) 28

LEAGUE GOALS
GERRY GOW
34

BRISTOL CITY
TEAM LEADERS

LEA. APPEARANCES
BRIAN DRYSDALE 271

BIG FEE MAN
CHRIS GARLAND £110,000

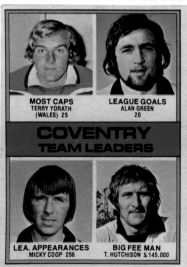

MOST CAPS
TERRY YORATH
(WALES) 25

LEAGUE GOALS
ALAN GREEN
20

COVENTRY
TEAM LEADERS

LEA. APPEARANCES
MICKY COOP 256

BIG FEE MAN
T. HUTCHISON £145,000

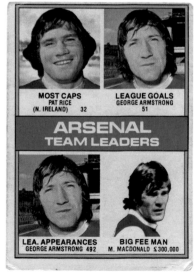

MOST CAPS
PAT RICE
(N. IRELAND) 32

LEAGUE GOALS
GEORGE ARMSTRONG
51

ARSENAL
TEAM LEADERS

LEA. APPEARANCES
GEORGE ARMSTRONG 492

BIG FEE MAN
M. MACDONALD £300,000

Topps 1976–77

TOPPS ALL★STARS

GORDON McQUEEN
DEFENDER • SCOTLAND

TOPPS ALL★STARS

LIAM BRADY
MIDFIELDER • EIRE

TOPPS ALL★STARS

TERRY YORATH
MIDFIELDER • WALES

TOPPS ALL★STARS

SANDY JARDINE
DEFENDER • SCOTLAND

Topps 1978–79

JIM PLATT
MIDDLESBROUGH

FRANK LAMPARD
WEST HAM

GEORGE BEST
FULHAM

DAVE McCULLOCH
AYR

Topps 1976–77

Top Trumps

The card game that dominated sales in the 1970s was Waddington's Top Trumps. Unlike most other football card games, it managed to be both playable and collectable. The company didn't concentrate merely on football, though, as Top Trumps issued sets on everything from planes to tanks to 'horror creatures'. The game itself was very simple. Each card depicted a player and some of his statistics, such as height, weight, games played and goals scored. You challenged your opponent on one of these stats and if your card had the higher figure you won their card.

The first football set was *British Soccer Stars* in 1978 (expect to pay a pound a card nowadays), which was quickly followed by *World Cup 78*, then more *British Stars* in 1980 and 1982. Some of the most sought-after cards at the moment are the limited team sets that were issued in the early 1980s. If you found a complete set with the small badge that came with it you would probably have to pay more than £25 for it.

Top Trumps seemed to die out during the 1980s, but they made a half-hearted comeback between 1995 and 97, when a variation called Subbuteo cards was issued each season. Ultimately the brand was sold to Winning Moves in the 1990s, who have revitalised the series. They can now be found on shop counters up and down the country again. At the time of

Chelsea
Ray 'Butch' Wilkins

International Appearances	9
International Goals	0
League Appearances	125
League Goals	22
Height	5' 7"

West Germany
Sepp Maier

World Cup Appearances	12
World Cup Goals	0
International Appearances	79
International Goals	0
Height	6' 0"

writing, a new Top Trumps football series titled *European Football Stars* was being prepared for issue, featuring the likes of Henry, Beckham and Zidane in place of Keegan, Vogts and Platini.

Argentina 1978

Despite England's failure to qualify, the 1978 World Cup was well covered by all the usual card issuers. Topps produced a sub-set depicting all the previous World Cup finals but managed to use a picture of Alan Ball for the 1974 West Germany–Holland final! Panini and FKS issued their usual album and sticker sets. The previously unknown Monty Gum Company arrived on the scene with a poorly produced set that had blank-backed cards. Even Golden Wonder jumped on the bandwagon.

Scotland thought they had an 'easy' group, comprising Peru and Iran as well as one of the favourites, Holland. They proceeded to lose 3–1 to Peru and could only hold the Iranians to a draw. Ironically, they then beat the mighty Dutch, who would go all the way to a ticker-tape final before being cut down by the cynical hosts. In the same tournament, the Brazilians disappointed despite some spectacular goals, the West German holders bowed out meekly after a loss to Austria, and the French gave a World Cup debut to a young maestro called Platini.

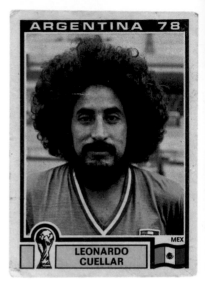

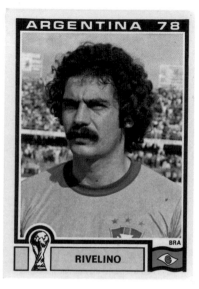

ARGENTINA 78

RIVELINO

BRA

ARGENTINA 78

BRUCE RIOCH

SCO

ARGENTINA 78

MARIO ALBERTO KEMPES

ARG

ARGENTINA 78

MICHEL PLATINI

FRA

Mistakes on Cards

If all the mistakes, changes and alternative versions of cards and stickers over the years were listed, they would fill this book. Errors include the wrong picture, the wrong caption or incorrect information on the back, as well as ink-errors and mis-cutting of the cards. A whole sub-genre of serious collectors has emerged to hunt down these error-strewn cards as they are usually much rarer than the correctly produced versions.

In the examples shown on p.132 the manufacturers could be partly forgiven, as brothers Jimmy and Brian Greenhoff do look quite similar. But mistaking some unknown goalie for England's most capped international is surely a mistake too far! Look closely at the card on the [right]. Is that really Peter Shilton?

The worst-case scenario for the manufacturers was of course when a player was transferred after the designs had been sent to the printers. Alex Cropley's move from Arsenal to Aston Villa seems to have caused some last-minute alterations to his shirt. The same was true for Archie Gemmill (see overleaf) after he left Derby County for Nottingham Forest. Yet another coat of paint and here he is in the Scotland line-up.

Another task for the collector is to track down variations of cards that were changed by the manufacturer in mid-season. Most of these changes seem to have been made on a whim. For example, the rear of the Roger Morgan cards (overleaf) are identical, but then someone must have decided that we really should see him in close-up. The close-up shot is worth more than double the earlier card. John Sissons, meanwhile, seems to have aged about ten years between the two photographs used on his card. In this case the text on the back of the card has also been altered. The one in which he looks older will set you back five times the price of the other card!

The David Sadler cards are especially unusual in that not only did the photo change mid-season (for no apparent reason) but the rear of the card was also revamped. The player biography was shortened, the 'football quiz' changed and even Sadler's place of birth moved several miles from Maidstone to Yalding.

DAVID SADLER
MANCHESTER UNITED

CENTRE
HALF

DAVID SADLER
MANCHESTER UNITED

CENTRE
HALF

TOPPS SALUTES

PETER SHILTON

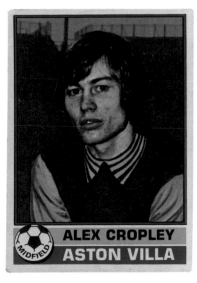

MIDFIELD

ALEX CROPLEY
ASTON VILLA

JOHN SISSONS
WEST HAM UNITED

OUTSIDE
LEFT

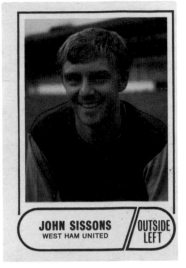

JOHN SISSONS
WEST HAM UNITED

OUTSIDE
LEFT

BRIAN GREENHOFF

JIMMY GREENHOFF

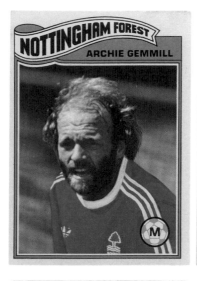

NOTTINGHAM FOREST

ARCHIE GEMMILL

M

TOPPS SCOTLAND
★ ALL-STARS ★

1978
WORLD
CUP
ENTRY

midfielder **ARCHIE GEMMILL**

TOTTENHAM

WINGER

ROGER MORGAN

TOTTENHAM

WINGER

ROGER MORGAN

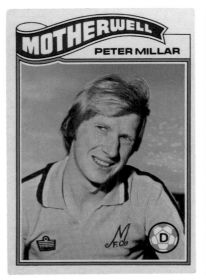

MOTHERWELL
PETER MILLAR

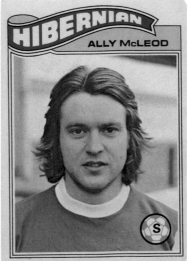

HIBERNIAN
ALLY McLEOD

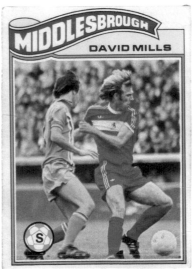

MIDDLESBROUGH
DAVID MILLS

NOTTINGHAM FOREST
JOHN ROBERTSON

Topps 1977–78

KEN SANSOM

CRYSTAL PALACE

PETER WARD

BRIGHTON

ARNOLD MUHREN

IPSWICH

RICARDO VILLA

TOTTENHAM

Topps 1978–79

The 1980s and Beyond

Rubbish 1980s

Let's face it, Britain in the 1980s was rubbish. The whole country seemed to be on a downward spiral as the decade progressed. The iron hand of Thatcherism, social unrest, the miners' strike and some truly atrocious music all contributed to creating a depressing decade. And football didn't help. Rampant racism and violence on the terraces, the Bradford fire, Heysel and Hillsborough left a sick feeling in the pit of every football fan's stomach. No wonder attendances were plummeting. To top it all, football kits were at their most hideous and haircuts were abominable; even the shirt sponsors seemed to be awful.

For the collector it was a barren time, too. Cards had been phased out almost completely, aside from the annual Barrett/Bassett set. Panini was ready to be sold off to the Maxwell Group.

GARY LINEKER

DAVID SEAMAN

TOTTENHAM HOTSPUR

OSVALDO ARDILES

ALEC FERGUSON MANAGER

LEICESTER CITY

IND COOPE

ANDY FEELEY

LAURIE CUNNINGHAM

SAM ALLARDYCE

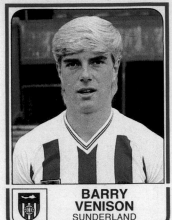

BARRY VENISON
SUNDERLAND

PAUL STURROCK

MARTIN O'NEILL
NOTTS COUNTY

WEST BROMWICH

BRYAN ROBSON

PETER REID
BOLTON WANDERERS

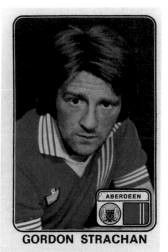

GORDON STRACHAN

ABERDEEN

MARK LAWRENSON
BRIGHTON & HOVE ALBION

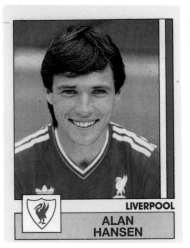

LIVERPOOL

ALAN
HANSEN

PAUL
GASCOIGNE

NEWCASTLE UNITED

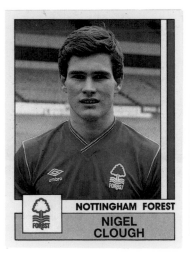

NOTTINGHAM FOREST

NIGEL
CLOUGH

GARTH
CROOKS

CHARLTON ATHLETIC

Larger format stickers appeared in Spain and formed quite impressive collections, even though some of the pictures seemed to have been taken in the players' back gardens.

JUAN CARLOS
R. SPORTING DE GIJON

FNDO. HIERRO
REAL MADRID C. DE F.

BRIAN CLOUGH

MIDDLESBROUGH

BRIAN CLOUGH
NOTTINGHAM FOREST

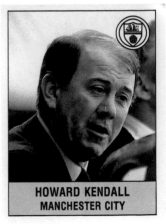

HOWARD KENDALL
MANCHESTER CITY

GRAHAM TAYLOR
LINCOLN CITY

BIRMINGHAM CITY

SIR ALF RAMSEY (Manager)

ENGLAND

GRAHAM
TAYLOR

Players who became managers

The 1990s

The Man U and Arsenal Years

The dawn of the Premiership in 1992–93 saw the last fling of the trade large card-size series of football cards. Pro Set had taken over the mantle that Topps had vacated in 1981 and issued vast sets of cards covering all manner of clubs.

The early 1990s also saw the emergence of the Merlin Company (now part of the Topps Group) who produced both cards and stickers, and eventually won the exclusive rights to the Premiership. Card and sticker collecting was changing in much the same way as the game itself.

In the 1970s the old Division One League Championship was won by five different teams, while seven different clubs finished as runners-up. The gap between first and second was three points or less on seven occasions. In short, you could never be sure who would win the League or who would challenge them, and in most years the championship race would go right down to the wire. In the 1990s the advent of the Premier League changed all of that. The first nine years of the new competition saw Manchester United win the title seven times and come runners-up twice (by a single point each time), when Arsenal wrestled it away from Old Trafford and Blackburn bought it.

Old-style card-collecting all but died out for over a decade as the producers concentrated solely on the big clubs: Manchester United, Liverpool, Arsenal and Celtic fans were among the few who could now buy cards of their heroes.

Opposite page: a Bassett 1980s selection. Clockwise from top left: Noel Brotherston (Blackburn Rovers); Peter Beardsley (Newcastle United); Jasper (sic) Olsen (Manchester United); John Barnes (Watford); Stuart Pearce (Nottingham Forest); Gary Pallister (Middlesbrough)

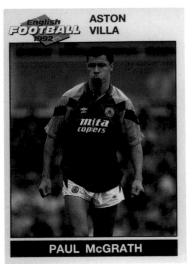

English FOOTBALL 1992

ASTON VILLA

PAUL McGRATH

MATTHEW LE TISSIER

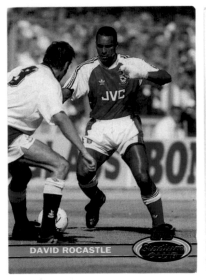

DAVID ROCASTLE

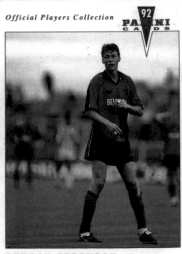

Official Players Collection

92 PANINI CARDS

DUNCAN FERGUSON

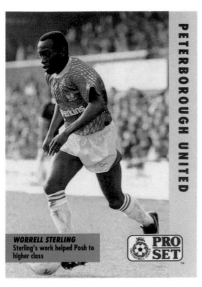

PETERBOROUGH UNITED

WORRELL STERLING
Sterling's work helped Posh to
higher class

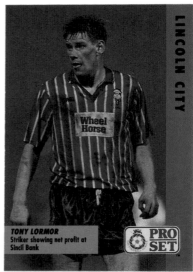

LINCOLN CITY

TONY LORMOR
Striker showing net profit at
Sincil Bank

IAIN DOWIE
SOUTHAMPTON

MALDINI Paolo

70

PAOLO MALDINI

Milano (ITA), 26.6.1968

1.87 m, 85 kg

Milan (ITA)

Italia

Defender

©1999 FIFA TM

Manufactured
under license by PANINI

RIVALDO

36

RIVALDO
Vitoria da Conquista
Recife (BRA), 19.4.1972

1.86 m, 75 kg

Barcelona (ESP)

Brasil

Forward

©1999 FIFA TM

Manufactured
under license by PANINI

Shoot Out! and the Revival of Card Games

With the amount of entertainment available to children today, it is somewhat surprising that the humble football card game has made a successful comeback in the twenty-first century. Magic Box's *Shoot Out!* trading card game has proved to be a big success, following in the footsteps of Pepys, A & BC, Top Trumps and even Subbuteo in the realm of football card games.

To start the collection you can purchase a special pack for £4.99, which includes cards, an A4 folder with integral plastic sleeves to hold the whole set of 18 players per Premiership side, and a playing board made from sturdy cardboard. The board has slots into which each player's team can be fitted, but the game's rules utterly bewildered this potential player. No doubt an average ten-year-old will be able to explain it to you in a couple of minutes.

2000s – New-style Stickers and Albums

While the situation has obviously progressed from the dark days of the eighties, there are still a lot of things wrong with football today. With all-seater stadia and astronomical ticket prices to watch pampered mercenaries who will move on to a bigger pay packet at the drop of a hat, it's now a

GOAL KICK Extra turn.

No. 17 IN A SET OF 22.

GORDON BANKS · STOKE CITY

GOAL KICK Extra turn.

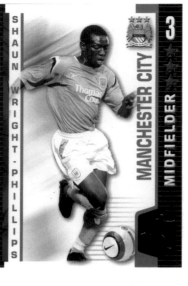

SHAUN WRIGHT-PHILLIPS

MANCHESTER CITY

3

MIDFIELDER

GOOD PASS Extra turn.

No. 4 IN A SET OF 22.

PETER OSGOOD · CHELSEA

GOOD PASS Extra turn.

CRISTIANO RONALDO

MANCHESTER UNITED

2

STRIKER

business more than a sport.
Jumpers for goal-posts it ain't.

Cards and stickers are still enjoying
their revival, though, with the
Premiership merchandising
machine rolling along relentlessly.
But whereas in days gone by the
kids would amass the cards of
players they watched from
windswept terraces on a Saturday
afternoon, today most of them are
collecting images of footballers
they've only ever seen on TV.

One of the obvious changes in the
game is evident on the front of
recent sticker issues. Not too long
ago a child could wait outside a
top-flight football ground after a
game and get his favourite players
to sign the cards he'd collected.
Today the players depart in their
Ferraris and BMWs from behind
cordoned-off areas and the kids
rarely get the chance to meet
them. So now the sticker
companies print the autographs
on the stickers. It's a sad illustration
of the way the game has stopped
being the people's sport to become
one played by millionaires and
watched by the wealthy.

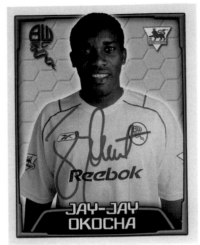

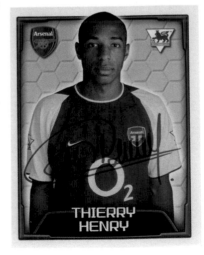

The Internet Boom

Unfortunately for my bank balance, the rediscovery of a stash of my old cards coincided with the launch of the internet and that dreaded four-letter word, eBay. Suddenly the card world was at your fingertips as they hovered above the keyboard. Did I really want to start filling the house with cards? My wife wasn't too keen on the excessive amounts of books, magazines, records and CDs that already took up far too much room. And it wasn't very likely that she would be thrilled by the idea of filling up those 23 spaces left in the Panini *Football 79* album that had been gathering dust for years.

But I was!

On eBay the choice of cards is truly amazing. Bargains can be had if three or four copies of the same card happen to be listed at the same time. Equally, of course, if dozens of people around the globe are chasing one particular lot, the bids can go through the roof. You have to be able to pick and choose, know when to dive in and when to hold back because the same card might be up for sale again the following week.

Auctions and Card Fairs Today

You can boost your collection of cards, and sometimes stickers, at one of the many auctions that take place around the country. There are some specialist card auctions, but many general sporting memorabilia auctions now also feature lots of cards due to the spiralling prices.

Lots are usually available for inspection the day before the auction, often in large cardboard boxes filled to the brim with part-sets of stickers, albums and cards in all extremes of condition. Careful perusal of the lots beforehand could lead you to a bargain, but of course many other collectors know this trick, too.

At a recent auction a box of about 20 sticker albums, filled to varying degrees, came under the hammer. I thought I might be in with a chance if I went up to £200. It eventually sold for more than £700! I was more successful with some smaller lots that seemed to be of no interest to most bidders, even though they turned out to be mini-treasure troves of cards.

Trevor Vennett-Smith runs auctions in the Nottingham area and often has sales dedicated to cigarette cards. 'In a recent sale we had a hundred and twenty people in the same room,' he says. 'All of them were here for cigarette cards.'

The Grading of Cards

For serious collectors, the quality of a card is crucial. Unfortunately, though, there are no hard and fast rules as to what a particular description means in reality. With the advent of mass sales over the internet, you could find yourself buying something in a far worse condition than you'd expected if you're not careful.

The main factors to look at when grading a card are: condition of the corners; surface condition (scratches, stains, creases); edge wear; centring of the image; print quality.

Here is a basic guide to grades:

Poor – A card that displays any of the following: creases and/or tears, badly rounded corners, has been removed from an album or is mis-cut. A card in this condition is worth a tiny fraction (usually less than a tenth, unless it is an extremely rare example) of any catalogue price.

Fair – A card in this condition will have signs of heavy use on its corners and edges, be badly centred or have damage to the reverse.

Good – These cards are OK as fillers for your collection, but have obviously been around the block a few times and usually have rounded corners.

Poor/Fair

Good

Very Good – Worth about 50 per cent of the catalogue value, these show signs of moderate handling, contain slight edge markings and will have lost some of the gloss from the front of the card.

Excellent – Many collectors ignore anything below this grade. If the card has one of the following it will fall from 'Near Mint' into this category: more than two slightly rounded corners; less than perfect centring; more than a slight loss of gloss; ink spots from the printing process.

Near Mint – Worth about 80–90 per cent of the 'Mint' price, a card in this category should have only one minor flaw visible.

Mint – Unfortunately, this grade is used far too often because the vast majority of cards do not merit it. In theory, as soon as a card has been taken from its packet it ceases to be 'Mint'. This description should therefore only be used in extreme circumstances.

These are not the 'official' gradings listed by the Cartophilic Society, which lists just five grades: Excellent, Very Good, Good, Fair and Poor. But such a short range of descriptions gives rise to many arguments and accusations. At a recent fair I was a bystander while a stall-holder and customer had a heated debate over the condition of a card and how that should affect its price compared to the catalogue listing.

The problem with all of these descriptions is that, for example, a card classed as 'Good' will by definition still have a number of faults. If someone has just inherited a box of old cards and rushed them on to eBay, their (often quite innocent) descriptions are likely to annoy serious collectors. So, when buying online, be sure to ask the seller questions, and if the scan is inadequate ask for a better one to be forwarded.

Any pricing given to cards should clearly state what grading is expected due to the card's age. For example, a card from before the First World War is very unlikely to have survived in anything better than 'Very Good' condition. Card catalogues often list what should be taken only as the worth of a card in the best condition that can be expected. For more recent cards, this would mean that the card could be available in 'Near Mint' condition today.

You should be aware that catalogues frequently underestimate the worth of certain highly desirable players and teams. Also, the first and last card of a set is often harder to find in 'Near Mint' condition, because, as they are usually kept at the top and bottom of the stack, they are likely to have suffered more wear and tear than the rest of the cards.

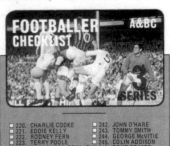

FOOTBALLER CHECKLIST A&BC

3 SERIES

☐ 220. CHARLIE COOKE	☐ 242. JOHN O'HARE
☐ 221. EDDIE KELLY	☐ 243. TOMMY SMITH
☐ 222. RODNEY FERN	☐ 244. GEORGE McVITIE
☐ 223. TERRY POOLE	☐ 245. COLIN ADDISON
☐ 224. MALCOLM MacDONALD	☐ 246. DOUG FRASER
☐ 225. NORMAN HUNTER	☐ 247. CYRIL KNOWLES
☐ 226. RAY CLEMENCE	☐ 248. COLIN DOBSON
☐ 227. ALAN DURBAN	☐ 249. ARTHUR MANN
☐ 228. JIMMY HUSBAND	☐ 250. BOBBY TAMBLING
☐ 229. MIKE ENGLAND	☐ 251. JOHN SJOBERG
☐ 230. ALAN BLOOR	☐ 252. TONY DUNNE
☐ 231. ASA HARTFORD	☐ 253. GERRY CONROY
☐ 232. GARY BELL	☐ 254. PAUL REANEY
☐ 233. ALAN HUDSON	☐ 255. JOHN McGARTH
☐ 234. PAUL MADELEY	☐ 256. BOBBY HOWE
☐ 235. JOHN CRAGGS	☐ 257. NEIL MARTIN
☐ 236. COLIN VILJOEN	☐ 258. ALAN MERRICK
☐ 237. BOB McNAB	☐ 259. ALAN MULLERY
☐ 238. GERRY QUEEN	☐ 260. FRANK PARSONS
☐ 239. PETER SHILTON	☐ 261. PETER MORRIS
☐ 240. ERNIE HUNT	☐ 262. EMLYN HUGHES
☐ 241. JIMMY LAWSON	☐ 263. DAVE CLEMENTS

© A&BC

TOPPS FOOTBALLER CHECKLIST
Cards 133-220

133	☐ Derek Parkin	147	☐ Duncan Forbes
134	☑ Stuart Pearson	148	☐ George Armstrong
135	☑ Peter Cormack	149	☐ Steve Seargeant
136	☑ Bob McNab	150	☑ Sammy McIlroy
137	☐ Mike Lyons	151	☐ Micky Droy
138	☐ Ron Harris	152	☑ Ray Kennedy
139	☐ Alfie Conn	153	☑ Paul Reaney
140	☑ Asa Hartford	154	☑ Kevin Keelan
141	☐ Roger Hynd	155	☐ Joe Kinnear
142	☑ Don Masson	156	☑ Stan Bowles
143	☑ Phil Thompson	157	☐ Frank Munro
144	☑ Geoff Salmons	158	☐ Mick Lambert
145	☐ George Burley	159	☑ Tommy Booth
146	☐ Mike Bailey	160	☑ Allan Mullery

TOPPS FOOTBALLER CHECKLIST
Cards 1-132

1 ☐ Billy Bremner		32 ☐ Check List: 1-132
2 ☐ Colin Waldron		33 ☐ John Radford
3 ☐ Jim Pearson		34 ☐ David Nish
4 ☐ Cyril Knowles		35 ☐ Alan Hudson
5 ☐ Trevor Francis		36 ☐ Martin Buchan
6 ☐ Henry Newton		37 ☐ Bobby Kerr
7 ☐ Brian Kidd		38 ☐ Frank McLintock
8 ☐ Stewart Houston		39 ☐ Jimmy Smith
9 ☐ John Mahoney		40 ☐ Kevin Keegan
10 ☐ Malcolm Macdonald		41 ☐ John Hollins
11 ☐ Bobby Moncur		42 ☐ Kevin Beattie
12 ☐ Dave Clement		43 ☐ Bobby Owen
13 ☐ Steve Heighway		44 ☐ Willie Carr
14 ☐ Allan Hunter		45 ☐ Jimmy Husband
15 ☐ Terry Yorath		46 ☐ Eddie Colquhon
16 ☐ Brian Alderson		47 ☐ Jim Cumbes
17 ☐ Charlie Aitken		48 ☐ Steve Earle
18 ☐ Mike Summerbee		49 ☐ Doug Collins
19 ☐ Len Badger		50 ☐ Mike Channon
20 ☐ Leighton James		51 ☐ Steve James
21 ☐ Iam McFaul		52 ☐ Brian Hall
22 ☐ Jon Sammels		53 ☐ Alan Foggon
23 ☐ Charlie Cooke		54 ☐ Billy Bonds
24 ☐ John Hurst		55 ☐ Roger Kenyon
25 ☐ Colin Viljoen		56 ☐ Martin Chivers
26 ☐ John Hickton		57 ☐ Johnny Giles
27 ☐ Frank Lampard		58 ☐ Rodney Marsh
28 ☐ Willie Donachie		59 ☐ Colin Todd
29 ☐ Steve Perryman		60 ☐ Peter Shilton
30 ☐ Paul Madeley		61 ☐ Howard Kendall
31 ☐ Gordon Taylor		62 ☐ Don Givens

Footballer CHECKLIST
CARDS 221-330

221 Gerry Keegan		247 Bobby Kerr
222 Jimmy Nicholl		248 David Peach
223 Stuart Barrowclough		249 John Matthews
224 David Stringer		250 Emlyn Hughes
225 Leighton James		251 Mel Holden
226 Jim Montgomery		252 Terry McDermott
227 Mick Leach		253 Allan Clarke
228 Willie Maddren		254 Phil Boyer
229 Chris McGrath		255 Paul Jones
230 Martin Peters		256 Roy Greaves
231 Peter Taylor		257 George Telfer
232 Kevin Lewis		258 Ray Kennedy
233 Jim McCalliog		259 Bryln Hamilton
234 Peter Noble		260 Willie Young
235 Bob Hatton		261 Francis Lee
236 Jim Platt		262 Eddie Gray
237 Mike Bernard		263 Ian Hamilton
238 Mick Lambert		264 Ken McNaught
239 Larry Lloyd		265 Gordon Hill
240 John Mahoney		266 John Radford
241 John Craggs		267 Dennis Mortimer
242 Terry Yorath		268 Alan Birchenall
243 Irving Nattrass		269 Alan Campbell
244 Mick McGuire		270 Norman Hunter
245 Mel Machin		271 Barry Powell
246 Jimmy Robertson		272 Joe Bolton

Postscript

I recently found myself surfing eBay on a Saturday morning. I wasn't looking for anything in particular, but I saw a sealed box of *Euro 2004* stickers at the 'buy-it-now' bargain price of just £2.50. I made the purchase and went off for a cup of tea. On returning to my computer I had a message from the seller. It turned out that they lived just a mile down the road, so they asked if I wanted to pop round and pick up the parcel. I jumped into the car and returned home a few minutes later with not one but two boxes of stickers. My afternoon was spent opening packet after packet of stickers.

What hit me first was the smell: not of the stickers, but of the two sticks of bubblegum that were in every packet. Then I set to carefully arranging the stickers in the album, something I hadn't done for almost a quarter of a century. I must admit that the first few were a little lopsided, but gradually I improved.

I was about to finish my first album since 1982 when disaster struck. After opening the last packet I was still one sticker short! So if anyone has a spare Merlin *Euro 2004* sticker 'EN2', please email me at robj@innotts.co.uk. I've got plenty of swaps to offer!

Bibliography

Ambrosen, Tony
The Illustrated Footballer
Breedon Books
Derby
1989

Howsden, Gordon
Collecting Cigarette & Trade Cards
New Cavendish Books
London
1995

Murray, Martin
The Story of Cigarette Cards
Murray Cards
London
1987

Thompson, David
Half-Time
Murray Cards
London
1987

Thanks and Acknowledge-ments

Many thanks to the following individuals and organisations for helping with the research and assembly of this book and for reproduction of the images: Gwyneth Glascodine at Futera International, IPC, Calum Laird and Pauline Morton at D. C. Thomson, Ged Wright, Match Day Cards, Mick Murphy, Murray Cards, NI Syndication, Alex Parsons at John Player/ Imperial Tobacco, Topps/Merlin, Vennett-Smith Auctions, Mark Warsop at Panini, Jon and Kjell at non-format and, of course, eBay! I must also thank Ian Preece at Orion books, though I am suspicious that he only commissioned this book so I could help him finish his FKS 1974–75 album! Every effort has been made to contact the copyright holders of the images in this book. Any enquiries concerning this please contact the publishers.

FOOTBALLER CHECKLIST SERIES ONE

1

1. RAY KENNEDY
2. CHRIS GARLAND
3. RODNEY MARSH
4. FRANK CLARK
5. DAVID LAWSON
6. ALEX STEPNEY
7. TREVOR CHERRY
8. KEVIN KEEGAN
9. CHRIS CATTLIN
10. TONY HAZELL
11. TREVOR BROOKING
12. CLIVE PAYNE
13. ERIC MARTIN
14. MIKE PEJIC

15. KEVIN HECTOR
16. JOHN JACKSON
17. TONY WANT
18. ALLAN HUNTER
19. PAT JENNINGS
20. BOBBY MOORE
21. TED HEMSLEY
22. ALAN WOODWARD
23. PETER OSGOOD
24. ALANBIRCHENALL
25. JOHN RADFORD
26. PETER SHILTON
27. MIKE DOYLE
28. STEWART BARROWCLOUGH

29. HOWARD KENDALL
30. IAN MOORE
31. ALLAN CLARKE
32. LARRY LLOYD
33. DENNIS MORTIMER
34. DAVE CLEMENT
35. GRAHAM PADDON
36. CHECKLIST 1
37. BOB McCARTHY
38. JOHN MARSH
39. ROY McFARLAND
40. ALAN WHITTLE
41. JOHN ROBERTS
42. KEVIN BEATTIE
43. MARTIN CHIVERS
44. JOHN McDOWELL

No. 246
Rob Jovanovic
Forward
Born: Nottingham
Ht. 5.10
Wt. 12st
Age 36

An enthusiastic player who notched 12 goals in the 1979–80 season as St Augustine's finished runners-up in the league.

Takes his football seriously, hence the shin-pads being worn for the team photo.

Was given a free transfer at the end of the season when he moved up to Christ the King comprehensive school.

Went on to write books about Nottingham Forest's European adventures, Beck, R.E.M, Pavement, Big Star and Nirvana.

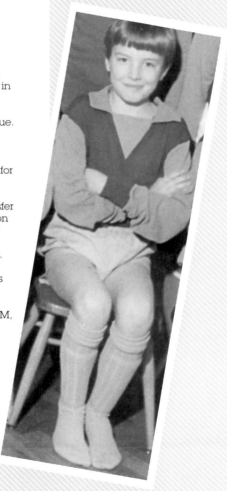